Religious liberty in the workplace

A guide for Christian employees

Mark Jones

CHRISTIAN INFLUENCE IN A SECULAR WORLD

Copyright © The Christian Institute 2008

The author has asserted his right under Section 77 of the Copyright, Designs & Patents Act 1988 to be identified as the author of this work.

First printed in February 2008

ISBN 978-1-901086-40-9

Published by The Christian Institute
Wilberforce House, 4 Park Road, Gosforth Business Park,
Newcastle upon Tyne, NE12 8DG

All rights reserved

No part of this publication may be reproduced, or stored in a retrieval system, or transmitted, in any form or by any means, mechanical, electronic, photocopying, recording or otherwise, without the prior permission of The Christian Institute.

The Christian Institute is a Company Limited by Guarantee, registered in England as a charity.
Company No. 263 4440, Charity No. 100 4774.
A charity registered in Scotland. Charity No. SC039220.

Contents

Introduction	5
The law	6
Particular considerations for Christians	9
Guidance referred to	11

Can I send Christmas cards to my colleagues?	12
Should I be allowed time off because of Church Services/Christmas/Easter?	13
Can I wear a cross?	14
I am being asked to wear an immodest uniform – can I refuse?	16
Can I share my faith in the workplace?	16
Can I give a Christian opinion on controversial topics?	17
I am worried I might be accused of being homophobic.	18
Can I object where my employer has asked me to undertake duties that are contrary to my Christian conscience?	20
My employer has asked me to provide a good or service for a client that is contrary to my Christian conscience.	20
How should I convey my concerns?	22

Conclusion	24

Dear reader,

As a lawyer who has advised Christians on a number of workplace issues, I have been asked to produce this guide for The Christian Institute. This guide sets out my views based upon the law and my understanding of the issues from those who have approached me. Within it I have tried to anticipate some of the situations that individual Christians may come across in the workplace and welcome guidance on. It does not seek to address issues that Christian organisations or those run in accordance with a Christian ethos may face.

This advice cannot be a definitive statement on the law and specific advice should always be sought on individual circumstances.

Yours faithfully,

Mark Jones
ORMERODS

Green Dragon House 64-70 High Street Croydon CR0 9XN
Telephone: 020 8686 5000; Fax: 020 8680 0972
e-mail: mark.jones@ormerods.co.uk www.ormerods.co.uk

The law

I do not propose setting out in full detail the legal provisions as they inform this advice, but an understanding of the basics may assist:

Contract law

All employees and workers provide their services to their employer under a contract, whether there is something in writing or not. In its most basic form, that contract is that the individual performs services required by the employer and the employer pays the individual.

Certain terms are implied into contracts. For employees, there is an implied term of mutual trust and confidence, which can be understood to mean that an employer should not without reasonable and proper cause conduct itself in a manner calculated (or likely) to seriously damage the relationship of mutual confidence and trust between employer and employee. An example of this would be an inappropriate threat of dismissal unless an employee's complies with an employer's wishes.

An employer's internal policies and procedures may form part of an individual's contract or may simply be advisory. All employers are obliged to have a grievance procedure allowing staff to raise formal concerns, and are obliged to provide details of that policy in writing within 2 months of your employment commencing.

Human Rights

Human Rights legislation protects the freedom to hold Christian views and beliefs and the freedom to manifest those beliefs in actions. However, whilst the right to hold the belief is absolute, the right to manifest it is qualified, that is it can be constrained by matters such as the rights of others. It is a "balancing act". That said, any employer who attempted to force an employee to act against their core religious beliefs would run the risk of breaking the law.

Human Rights legislation is not directly enforceable upon private organisations (as opposed to state bodies), but the Courts and Tribunals as state bodies must ensure their decisions are consistent with the legislation (making it indirectly enforceable).

Discrimination Law

There are specific discrimination laws that set out protections and rights for individuals based upon their Christian faith and beliefs.

There are 4 basic sub-divisions of discrimination:

a) Direct discrimination would be where a Christian is subjected to less favourable treatment purely because of their faith. For example, you are the only person not invited to a works function because it is believed your Christian beliefs would impede others from "enjoying themselves".

b) Indirect discrimination would be where an employer operates a provision criterion or practice that is not directly discriminatory but that puts Christians (and you) at a disadvantage. For example if all works functions are scheduled to take place on Sundays and you therefore feel unable to attend. A potential defence to indirect discrimination is to show that, even taking into account your concerns, the practice is "objectively justifiable". This means that there is a legitimate purpose behind the policy and that the chosen method is a proportionate means of achieving it. Therefore if the legitimate purpose was to boost staff morale, the Company would have to show that addressing this by only having functions on a Sunday was not using an inflexible hammer to crack a nut.

c) Victimisation would be where, having taken steps relating to concerns about discrimination (for example raising a grievance or supporting a colleague's concerns), you are then subjected to less favourable treatment as a result. An example would be if, having raised your concerns about work functions always being on Sundays and the difficulty this causes you as a Christian, you are then given a bad appraisal for not being a "team player".

d) Harassment would be where because of your faith you are subjected to unwanted conduct that violates your dignity or creates a working environment that is intimidating, hostile, degrading, humiliating or offensive for you. For example, colleagues ignore you because you never attend any of the Sunday work functions. In deciding whether or not the conduct is harassment, the question is whether having regard to all the circumstances including in particular your perception, it should reasonably be considered as having that effect. Reasonableness protects employers from being held liable on the whim of an unduly sensitive complainant.

Similar rights protect others on the grounds of their religious beliefs (including absence of belief) and some whose sexual lifestyle may be seen as conflicting with Biblical teaching and Church tradition. This creates conflicts. It is the unenviable task of an employer to juggle these conflicts and the guidance on how to do so is often unclear. Often these conflicts are resolved by decisions in the Courts and Tribunals, which may set precedents as to the correct approach if a similar conflict arises.

In relation to sexual lifestyle, there are provisions that protect individuals from being subjected to less favourable treatment because they are sexually attracted to persons of the same sex or both sexes. This applies to colleagues you may deal with and customers/third parties you may be expected to serve as part of your duties.

Particular considerations for Christians

Particularly in relation to human rights, harassment and indirect discrimination it is worth appreciating that actions of individuals can affect the balancing act mentioned above. If the impact of a practice on a Christian is seen as minor or they are considered unduly sensitive then there is less chance of there being a legal remedy. Sadly this is where our willingness as Christians to tolerate things that are wrong causes problems. For example, if we are too timid and take no exception to blasphemy in the workplace, the more likely it is that the isolated person who does take exception can be dismissed as unduly sensitive.

The more people know what Christians believe and expect Christians to profess their beliefs, the greater the prospects of society adapting. A community that allows itself to be offended without usually protesting is less able to objectively demonstrate offence when it chooses to protest.

This is not to suggest any form of civil disobedience, but, for example, if there are things in a workplace that mock Christ then it is legitimate to ask an employer if it would equally tolerate an image mocking other religious figures.

If as Christians we go along with the view that it is unacceptable to say that certain things are sinful, displeasing to God and may have eternal consequences, the more we may become part of the problem: when someone does stick their head above the parapet it is more likely to appear extreme. For example, if we had zero tolerance of blasphemy, it would jar much more when someone did blaspheme than it does now in many workplaces.

There is also a vicious spiral: the less able or willing we are to teach others about our faith, the less it will be understood and the less it will be taken into account by employers as working practices develop. I believe we have a fundamental duty to be involved in educating and informing colleagues and employers and influencing the organisations we work in.

As a Christian I must consider whether I should be having an influence in my work place. Is there any reason why I cannot offer my experience as a Christian to my employer as it develops informed working practices? The stance is not necessarily one of confrontation but consultation and offering your services.

One further consideration when seeking to establish religious freedoms within a workplace is that under the law those freedoms may equally apply to other religions or belief systems. Therefore if your employer is willing to help you promote an activity of Christian worship, they may equally have to assist a colleague who wants to promote an activity of non-Christian worship.

Guidance referred to

Legal decisions

Decisions by a forum of first instance (which includes the Employment Tribunal) are not binding on other Courts, but are persuasive. Decisions by an appellate forum (such as the Employment Appeal Tribunal, the Court of Appeal and the House of Lords) are binding on every forum below them.

ACAS

ACAS is a statutory body that assists with the resolution of workplace disputes. It has produced a guide on "Religion or Belief and the Workplace" ("the ACAS Guide"). Although not legally binding (and, some have suggested, not sympathetic to Christians), the Guide is of persuasive value to those interpreting the law.

Department for Communities and Local Government

DCLG has produced "Guidance on New Measures to Outlaw Discrimination on Grounds of Sexual Orientation in the Provision of Goods, Facilities and Services" ("the DCLG Guidance"). Parallel religious guidance has also been produced by the DCLG.

Questions

I have set out below a number of potential scenarios. There is much overlap between the answers and common principles apply to many of them, so I would recommend reading everything rather than questions in isolation.

A. Can I send Christmas cards to my colleagues?

Yes. This is unlikely to cause a problem. If your employer introduces a policy that says not to, then the solution is not to disregard that policy but to challenge it by entering into a dialogue to understand what drives it, address any misconceptions and identify an acceptable solution.

If you were to single out people of other faiths and send cards only to them, or if a colleague has made it clear to you that they do not want to receive Christmas (or Easter) cards from you but you still send them one, then an allegation of harassment and/or indirect discrimination could be made against you.

Some organisations may take the view that their corporate Christmas cards should be "multi-faith" or non-Christian. I remember one year receiving a Christmas card from a lawyer I know in Canada saying "happy holidays" and the offence/dismay I felt at Jesus' excision from a card commemorating his incarnation. There is nothing to prevent you from suggesting to your employer that the cards it uses should honestly reflect the occasion. It may be worth explaining that a Christian could be offended by something else.

B. Should I be allowed time off because of Church Services/ Christmas/Easter?

Those who work in retail have specific protection under the Employment Rights Act 1996 and are able to serve written notice on their employer that they are not willing to work Sundays. Three months' notice must be given. This exemption does not apply for those who only work on Sundays. (The same protection also applies to those in the betting trades).

In Copsey v WWB Devon Clays Ltd the Court of Appeal (in a decision that binds Employment Tribunals) held that an employer had done everything it reasonably could to accommodate a Christian employee's desire not to work on Sundays (and that his dismissal was therefore not because of his faith but his refusal to accept a change to the shift pattern). This "reasonable accommodation" principle is an important one and is in addition to the discrimination protection (which came into force subsequently).

Cases decided under the discrimination legislation strengthen this position. In the cases of Williams-Drabble v Pathway Care Solutions Ltd, the Employment Tribunal held that it was unlawful indirect discrimination against a Christian to require all employees to work a shift pattern including Sundays. Although there may have been a legitimate reason behind the aim, the impact of the policy upon Mrs Williams-Drabble was excessive and therefore disproportionate in relation to the aim. A similar conclusion was reached by the Employment Tribunal in the case of Edge v Visual Security Services Limited.

In cases like this, the resources of the employer are important. A small employer will be more able to argue that it is unable to accommodate requests for different working patterns. An employer with several hundred employees will face a more difficult argument that it was not possible to accommodate. My view is that it is not an excuse for an employer to refuse a Christian's request to have time off at a particular time on the basis that that will open the floodgates, ie. that everyone will then claim they are a "Christian" and then ask for Christmas off. It is only if such a situation arises and causes a problem in practice that the employer may need to review the extent to which such requests are accommodated.

The ACAS Guide states (p32) that *"Staff may request annual leave to coincide with religious festivals. Refusal to grant such leave may be discriminatory if it cannot be justified by a legitimate business need which cannot be met by any other reasonable means."*

When submitting any such request it therefore makes sense to offer ways in which the request may be reasonably accommodated.

C. Can I wear a cross?

Generally speaking the answer has to be yes.

It would be direct discrimination if the only items of jewellery banned from a workplace were Christian symbols such as a cross or an icthus fish. It might be indirect discrimination if all jewellery was banned, depending upon the reasons.

To draw a parallel, in the case of Azmi v Kirklees MBC the Employment Appeal Tribunal (whose decisions bind Employment Tribunals) held that it was legitimate for a school to require a Muslim teaching assistant to remove her veil while in class. As it was all head coverings that obscured the face that were banned (so not exclusively applying to Muslims) it was not direct discrimination. As there was a legitimate purpose (to educate children) and the ban was held to be a proportionate means of achieving this there was no indirect discrimination.

There is less obviously a legitimate reason for banning jewellery that does not impact upon a person's duties. A health and safety risk may be suggested, but unless the risk is obvious, any perceived health and safety risk should be explained and should be understood as a consideration within the balancing act, rather than conclusive.

The ACAS Guide states (p33) that *"organisations should try to be flexible where they can to enable staff to dress in accordance with their beliefs but still meet the organisation's requirements"*.

It may be important for an employer to understand that, for a Christian, whilst an outward expression of their faith through specific clothing or jewellery may not be prescribed in the Bible, it is a tenet of their Christian faith to share that faith with others. They may choose to do this by wearing certain jewellery, publicly displaying to their colleagues the convictions they hold. Employers should realise that this is a considered way of doing so (one that perhaps avoids ways that could cause employers greater consternation). The employer who wants to ban such expressions should be prepared to enter into a dialogue of how the concerns leading to the ban can be addressed in a way that still permits such expression. For example, in R on application of SB v Headteacher & Governors of Denbigh High School the House of Lords held that a school could refuse to allow a Muslim schoolgirl to wear a full-length jilbab when it was prepared to allow her to wear a shalwar kameez, or other modest clothing.

If the employer's stance is that no such expressions are permitted then it is important that they understand the disproportionate impact this will have upon Christians who may feel that it is their duty to bear Christian witness.

If an employer has a diversity or similar policy, then this can be checked for compatibility. It strikes me that an organisation that forbids considered expressions of the Christian faith is not standing for diversity at all but rather a bland secular uniformity.

D. I am being asked to wear an immodest uniform – can I refuse?

If the objection is because of your faith, the reasoning set out in "C" above will apply. (There may also be an argument that an immodest uniform could amount to sex discrimination.)

It is worth adding that an employee will tend to be in a stronger position to ask for their faith to be accommodated if what is required of them (to which they object) has changed since their employment commenced, compared to someone who goes into a job knowing what is expected of them and working initially without protest. If an employee comes to faith whilst in the job and that leads to their concern, that would explain their previous acquiescence and put them in a slightly stronger position to object to an existing practice.

E. Can I share my faith in the workplace?

Generally speaking the answer has to be yes.

The Gospel is offensive and as Christians if we are going to share the Gospel we must anticipate that we will cause offence. This will bring us necessarily into conflict. The choices are: to avoid the risk of ever causing offence; be oblivious and indifferent to any offence that may be caused; or thoughtfully yet boldly find the middle ground.

Some employers may have a policy specifically forbidding discussions about faith, although this is rare. The ACAS Guide advises at p31 that "*a ban on discussions about [Christianity] may create more bad feeling amongst staff and cause more problems than it solves.*" If such a ban is in place, an appropriate step is to enter into a dialogue with the employer to understand the ban and its underlying concerns and see if these can be addressed in a way that will allow such discussions.

The concern will often be that other staff who do not share your faith may be made to feel uncomfortable.

However, the ACAS Guide also confirms that *"If harassment has been explained to staff they should be able to distinguish between reasonable discussion and offensive behaviour. Staff should be aware that if their discussions cause offence then this may be considered to be harassment..."*.

The ACAS Guide gives the specific question and answer example that *" 'A group of religious staff have started trying to persuade other employees to attend their church. An atheist has said that it makes him uncomfortable. What should we do?' The group's behaviour may amount to harassment, for which the company could be liable unless it takes steps as are reasonably practicable to prevent it. You should refer the employee to the grievance procedure in case he wishes to make a formal complaint. Even if he doesn't, it would be sensible to speak to the staff informally and explain that some people find their behaviour unwelcome"*.

In order not to fuel any such concerns about workplace discussions it is important to express your beliefs in a temperate way, bearing in mind your position. Someone in a managerial position may also be considered to have greater influence over staff and therefore expected to exercise greater discernment.

The last 2 paragraphs in "C" above may also be relevant here.

Furthermore, an employer may need to understand that an inability to discuss Christianity in the workplace is going to be conducive to a lack of understanding of the Christian faith and may well cause problems to arise through ignorance. For example, there may be an increased likelihood of language and conduct likely to unintentionally offend Christians if other employees are unaware of what Christians delight in or derive offence from.

F. Can I give a Christian opinion on controversial topics?

The legally "safe" advice would be to minimise any risk of ever creating a personal liability by never doing anything that someone could be offended by. As a Christian lawyer, I could not live by the standard that I would then be commending.

One Employment Tribunal has held that the fact that it is scripture being quoted does not provide a blanket defence to allegations that those views are offensive. Nevertheless, an employer should take into consideration whether an opinion is informed by your Christian beliefs and, if so, take that into account before deciding what response is appropriate.

One consequence of the legislation is that a person has better protection when expressing their views if those views derive from their Christian faith rather than someone whose views are not informed by their faith (or absence of faith).

A principle that can be extrapolated from the DCLG Guidance (see "G" below) is that it may be more acceptable to put something in the context of a personal view, for example "as a Christian, I believe that…" or "the Bible says that…" rather than stating something as a bold fact without a reference point for that view.

This should also encourage Christians to share their personal testimony with colleagues during such discussions, taking them on the journey travelled rather than just expressing a concluded view.

From an employer's perspective, dialogue between staff rather than confrontation maintains the desired working relationship.

G. I am worried I might be accused of being homophobic.

To an extent this follows on from "F" above.

My view is that the term "homophobic" should never properly be applicable to a Christian. Our words and actions should never derive from hatred or an irrational fear of those under any form of temptation, sexual or otherwise. However, it must be recognised that this is how expressing the Church's orthodox position on sexual sin may be perceived or described by some.

It may therefore be important to convey the context of any

particular view. For example, consider whether it is misleading to talk exclusively about homosexual sexual sin if you consider the biblical view to be that all sex outside marriage is sinful. It is also important that colleagues understand how your view is informed.

The DCLG Guidance (which is within the context of providing goods and services) states that "if a pupil asks a teacher his views on homosexuality and the teacher gives his view, then again, that teacher will not be acting unlawfully", although the way that view is conveyed could be inappropriate. If this is the view within schools in relation to a teacher pupil context, it should be all the more so in relation to discussions between colleagues who are peers.

Although it remains to be seen if this is what happens in practice, the FAQ within the DCLG Guidance (p33) says *"The Regulations [governing the provisions of goods and services] will not: i) enable someone to be sued for holding or expressing views about homosexuality or sexual relationships..."* However this does not mean that there may not be a breach of some other legal obligation, including an employer's own workplace standards and expectations.

If a Christian considers that there are workplace practices that promote homosexual issues and behaviour that they are uncomfortable with, (for example promotion of a workplace gay and lesbian society, fundraising for gay rights groups or diversity training that expresses the view that sexual orientation is exclusively a matter of nature), the starting point is to explain in advance to the employer the issue this creates. It is important to put this in a full context, so that you explain that you are a Christian and what you believe as a Christian, before going into specifics about what concerns you and why (and explaining how it is informed by your Christian faith). Then you can move on to make any suggestions that could help and finally refer to any company policy that means that you hope that your concern will be taken seriously and accommodated.

H. Can I object where my employer has asked me to undertake duties that are contrary to my Christian conscience?

Yes. Examples could include lying on someone else's behalf or being asked to work a lottery machine in a newsagent when you are opposed to gambling.

The same principle of reasonable accommodation set out in "B" above applies. If you have been targeted to undertake such duties precisely because of your faith, this is likely to be direct discrimination. In relation to indirect discrimination, it is questionable whether lying could be seen to be a legitimate aim, but if the duty you are being asked to undertake is a legitimate aim, as mentioned above, the need for you to undertake it must be proportionate to that aim.

Whilst continuing to act in a manner that is reasonable, you should object clearly, as soon as the request is made; be aware that the more you acquiesce in requests contrary to your conscience, the more difficult it may be to convince anyone of the strength of your religious convictions.

I. My employer has asked me to supply a good or service to a client that is contrary to my Christian conscience.

Where this relates to sexuality, again it must be appreciated that there are additional considerations due to the need to balance competing rights within discrimination law. In general terms, it would be unlawful to refuse to provide a service to an individual because of their sexual orientation or lifestyle. However, if in providing that service you would be compromising your Christian conscience it will be quite appropriate to ask for your conscience to be accommodated and it may be unlawful if your request is not properly taken on board.

For example, it may be possible to draw a valid distinction between a person who works at a printers who objects to providing any services to a homosexual (which should be assumed to be unlawful) and objecting as a matter of Christian conscience to printing flyers promoting homosexual sexual activity (in the belief that they would thereby be condoning behaviour anathema to their personal conscience). In such a case, a Christian may need to show consistency when asked to print material pertaining to heterosexual sexual activity which they similarly consider to be wrong (such as that outside marriage) or be able to justify any distinction drawn (which may not be straightforward).

Rights of religious conscience figured prominently in The Christian Institute's 2007 case against the Northern Ireland Sexual Orientation Regulations (The Christian Institute & Ors, Re Application for Judicial Review). In giving his decision, Mr Justice Weatherup referred favourably to the Canadian case of Ontario Human Rights Commission v Brockie. He summarised the approach to religious conscience in the Brockie case by saying that a believer is "not required to undertake action that promotes that which the essence of the belief teaches to be wrong". Although this case relates to the area of goods and services, the principle is just as applicable to an employment scenario.

On the DCLG website, in giving an overview of the DCLG Guidance, the DCLG states that "*individuals who are concerned that the requirements of their job may be incompatible with their religious beliefs may ask their employer to be redeployed. Employers should be sensitive to the religious beliefs and perspectives of their employees and will need to be mindful of their obligations under the [discrimination legislation] not to discriminate against their employees on grounds of religion or belief.*"

The above quote is specifically in relation to matters where there is a conflict between religious rights and matters of sexual orientation. The obligation to accommodate Christians will be stronger where the matter of conscience does not need to be balanced against rights relating to sexual orientation, such as where the printer is asked to print a flyer containing a blasphemous image.

J. How should I convey my concerns?

I would generally recommend putting concerns in writing, because it provides a clear record and also may enable you to express matters more fully and in a way that is not possible (or could be easily misunderstood) if expressed for the first time face-to-face. The approach should be one of informing and indeed educating an employer (who may be completely ignorant about what Christians believe) rather than confronting. This may be the first opportunity the person you write to will ever have had to hear the Gospel, so use the opportunity and privilege wisely.

As stated at the beginning, employees should have access to a grievance procedure and that is normally the appropriate first step.

A failure to adequately investigate or pursue an employee's grievance can amount to discrimination in itself, if the failure to deal properly with the complaint was itself due to religious reasons (extrapolating the principle from Eke v Commissioners of Customs & Excise).

There is also a more formal "Questionnaire" procedure. This allows workers to use a prescribed document to submit specific questions about their treatment and their concerns that it is discriminatory. If an employer fails to answer it or gives evasive answers, a Tribunal is likely to consider that reaction to be strong evidence in support of any claim.

Finally, it may be possible to pursue a remedy in the Employment Tribunal. Normally claims have to be brought within 3 months of the offending act. This should normally be the last resort.

It has to be understood that employers are given a certain amount of flexibility within the judicial process. There are employers who are sympathetic to Christians and there are employers who are hostile. Different decisions may be reached by different organisations facing similar circumstances and both may be equally justifiable in law. It is important to bear in mind that, in the event of a dispute, a third party may end up reading your communications. If a situation cannot be resolved and the correspondence shows an employee to have been reasonable in the face of an unreasonable employer, they are more likely to have the Tribunal's sympathy.

Conclusion

In a nutshell, it is important to understand that the employer who disregards your Christian beliefs has broken the law. The employer who considers your Christian beliefs and reaches a conclusion that is reasonable, albeit not the conclusion you were hoping for, is likely to have complied with the law in principle. The employer who accommodates every request Christians make may be breaking the law in its obligations to its other staff and/or its clients.

There is therefore undoubtedly the need for discernment and wise counsel, both spiritually and legally, in the concerns we raise and the manner in which we raise them. Pursuing an ill-founded complaint against a colleague or employer can be no less harmful a witness than acquiescing in ungodly conduct.

There are secular organisations that may be able to provide advice without charge, including ACAS (www.acas.org.uk) and the Citizens Advice Bureau, although this is unlikely to be advice with a specific Christian sentiment.

Miracles of and Happiness

Subhash Lakhotia

DIAMOND BOOKS

ISBN : 978-81-288-3614-5

© Author

Publisher	: **Diamond Pocket Books (P) Ltd.**
	X-30, Okhla Industrial Area, Phase-II
	New Delhi-110020
Phone	: 011-40712100, 41611861
Fax	: 011-41611866
E-mail	: sales@dpb.in
Website	: www.diamondbook.in
Edition	: 2012
Printed by	: **G.S.Interprises**

Miracles of Health and Happiness
By - Ram Kailash Gupta

Contents

Preface 5
1. It's Miracles Time to Experience the 8
   Health and Happiness
2. Vowels of Happiness 16
3. Your Kingdom of Joy with Your Happiness 22
4. Out from Anger Acid for Your Own Health and 30
   Happiness
5. Fear Psychosis 35
6. Adopt WAP Formula for Your Health and Happiness 38
7. Fast and Not Feast: the Mantra for Your Health 41
8. Getting Cured without the Medicines: 45
   Nature Cure Way
9. Be Vegetarian for Your Robust Health 51
10. Gita Saar: the Depression Remover 54
11. Happiness from MT: an Experience 56
12. Count Your Blessings and Be Happy 60
13. Visit a Hospital Lounge on Regular Basis to 62
    Reap the Fruits of Happiness
14. The Best Gift to Your Parents for Your Happiness 65
15. Be Contended to Be Happy 69
16. Special Birthday Feast for Your Happiness 72
17. Remove Depression with 'Japa' for 74
    Your Health and Happiness
18. Forming CCG Group for Your Happiness 77
19. Group Travel Trip for Your Happiness 80
20. Surgery for Your Happiness 85
21. The In-built Formula for Happiness 88
    in PC Programmes
22. Meditate on the Theme "Deserve versus 93
    Desire" and Be Happy
23. VRS for your Happiness 97
24. WATS: a Formula for Instant and 100
    Guaranteed Happiness
25. Faith in God Can Relieve Your Body Pain 103
    and Get Back Your Lost Happiness

26. Positive Thinking: a Yes Formula for Your happiness 105
27. Kaya Kalpa for Your Health 108
28. Avoid A3 for Your Own Health and Happiness 113
29. It Must Be Ready for Your Ego 117
30. Cancel Your Appointment with Mr. PHJ 119
31. Keep Formula FF in Your Crown 121
32. Meditate on Your Life Mission and Be Happy 123
33. The Blissful Silence for the Blissful Happiness 124
34. Don't Play with the Emotions of Others 127
35. Stop Show-off for Your Happiness 129
36. Psychosomatic Diseases Can Be Cured for Your Health and Happiness 133
37. Your Happiness Formula: Worry Not for All That Has Not Happened 135
38. Timely Legal Compliances Keep You Happy 140
39. WAP: Another Happiness Formula 142
40. Time to Buy Your Happiness 144
41. Chant and Be Happy 146
42. Fear Not for Your Own Health and Happiness 150
43. How to Be Happy under Unhappy Circumstances and Situations of Life 152
44. Superior Happiness 153
45. Social Networking Sites for Your Happiness 157
46. Snatching an Hour a Day Can Make You Happy 159
47. MCP Programme for Health and Happiness 160
48. Live in Today for Your Happiness 165
49. Inspiring Quotations on Happiness 169
50. Reward Yourself and Be Happy 211
51. Mediate on a Quotation and Be Happy 213
52. New Medical Research for Your Health 219
53. Change Your Attitude for Your Happiness 225
54. Why Should You Enter Unhappiness Zone Due to Action of Someone Else 227
55. Inspire Lives of Others and Be Happy 233
56. The Thrilling Happiness 235
57. Rainbow Tips on Health and Happiness 244

Preface

I am happy to present this new book entitled "Miracles of Health and Happiness." I am sure the book will definitely bring better health for all its readers and would provide extra happiness in their life. If we screen the history of happiness, we find that centuries ago also the theme of happiness was discussed and debated not by one but by many philosophers and other knowledgeable persons in the world. Long time back the happiness was described as under :

> Happy the man who, free from cares,
> Like men of old still works
> His father's fields with his own oxen,
> Encumbered by no debt.

Later on John Dryden described happiness as under:
> Happy the man, and happy he alone,
> Who can call today his own;
> He who secure within can say:
> Tomorrow do thy worst, for I have lived today.

Happiness as recorded in Matthew is as under :

> Happy/Blessed (makarios) are the poor in spirit, for theirs is
> the kingdom of heaven.
> Happy are those who mourn, for they will be comforted.
> Happy are the meek, for they will inherit the earth.
> Happy are those who hunger and thirst for righteousness, for
> they will be filled.
> Happy are the merciful, for they will receive mercy
> Happy are the pure in heart, for they will see God.

Happy are the peacemakers, for they will be called children of
God.

Happy are those who are persecuted for righteousness's sake,
for theirs is the kingdom of heaven. (Matthew 5:3-11)

Likewise happiness as recorded in Luke is as under:
Happy/Blessed are you who are poor, for yours is the kingdom
of God.

Happy are you who are hungry now, for you will be filled.

Happy are you who weep now, for you will laugh.

Happy are you when people hate you, and when they exclude
you, revile you, and defame you on account of the Son of
Man.

Rejoice in that day and leap for joy, for surely your reward is
great in heaven.... (Luke 6:20-23)

With the passage of time many people started believing that sin is pure unhappiness, forgiveness is pure happiness. There is also a difference between happiness and misery. The book entitled Art of Contentment written by Richard Allestree also throws some light on the contentment in the context of more happiness. In my journey in this world for the last sixty years I strongly believe that happiness lies within us all and that is the real dictum of receiving more and more of happiness in our life.

Joyful Science can bring happiness for you and

likewise helping without any expectation can bring unprecedented happiness to one and all. I have been attracted by the concept of happiness for the last two decades even since I started conducting special seminar on "Investment in Health and Happiness" in New Delhi. This seminar is regularly being conducted every alternate year and is very well attended by the elite of Delhi town.

I am confident and very much optimistic that all my readers of this book will definitely derive more happiness in their life. I will feel my efforts rewarded if this book can add extra ounce of happiness in their life. Those who are unhappy for them the book is going to bring double happiness as they walk through different pages of this book. I would be happy to receive from my readers new ideas of happiness experienced by them so that I can include them in the next edition of my book.

I am thankful to my friend Shri Narendra Kumar Verma, the publisher of the book for taking all the pains to publish this book in such a short time.

August 2011

Subhash Lakhotia

Lakhotia Niwas

S-228, Greater Kailash-II,

New Delhi – 110048.

Ph. 9810001665, 011-29215434

slakhotia@satyam.net.in

1. It's Miracles Time to Experience the Health and Happiness

For the last 16 years as Secretary General of the Investor's Club, we have been holding, every alternate year, a special power packed Seminar with the caption "Investment in Health and Happiness." At all such seminars in the past, hundreds of persons attending the seminar have been benefited and have appreciated the theme of the seminar namely—Health & Happiness. Generally, this seminar is conducted on 2nd October from 9 a.m. until 2 p.m. The entire group of participants attending the programme at the end this programme feel very happy. I am really inspired by the happiness of these participants, hence I thought of writing this book which will talk about the Miracles of Health & Happiness and the magic of Health & Happiness. Before we proceed further, I would like every reader of this book, to consistently think that Yes, in this life health as well as happiness are the real two pillars which enable a person to enjoy the bliss and peace in this world. More than 100 years ago Sigmund Freud, appreciated and recognised the importance of happiness.

I strongly also believe that the miracle of health and happiness lies in one single fact namely, increasing your longevity. Just remember that your money alone cannot be your longevity, rather your good health and the happiness which you process, will alone bring in more years to add to your longevity. Hence, for leading a wonderful life and to live, health and happiness continue to be two most important sought after achievements for every human being.

A little over two years ago, my mother was admitted in the Apollo Hospital, New Delhi. She stayed there for nearly 11 days. I was with her mot of the time. During this period of 11 days, I interacted with hundreds of people. The net summary of my interaction with patients as well as with the relative was that everyone was interested in best of health for self as well as for their relatives. Only when the health was good, it was possible to achieve an experience of happiness in life. The long hours spent by me in the hospital and with the visitors gallery really brought me closer to these hundred's of people whose mental state of affairs was exactly as that of mine. I found half of the people having greatly depression because of great health problem to their dear and loved ones. I was also in the same state of affairs. I was mentally broken, I was emotionally weak, I was depressed by self. Well, it is natural that one becomes depressed and feels broken down, especially when some very close to your heart is facing great severe chronic health problem. At that point of time, I learned a new lesson of life, namely the lesson of keeping a perfect health. Believe me, believe me, when I say that only when you are healthy you can enjoy happiness. An unhealthy man, come what may, cannot enjoy happiness. Hence the fact remains that you can yourself see the miracles of life if you are healthy because happiness embarrasses you only when you are healthy. If you really want to achieve and experience the great miracle of health & happiness then in the first place you must have total faith and loyalty to the dictum that the miracles of health and happiness are going to happen. What all you have is just experience these miracles of health and happiness in your own life and continue to enjoy life with the health and happiness entering your life.

You are unhappy; you find in your life no reason to be happy about. You find yourself burdened with the problem of this life. You are interested to share some of your thoughts, some of your problem, some of your thinking, but the question arises with whom to share? The Hello ! Friend's era is now on. You may have dozens of your friends, but if tell you to write down a list of your closest friends, you can in one minute note down a big list of 10-20 or may be more friends of yours. But unfortunately, the real paradox is this that out of this list of your friends, to how many friends are you able to tell your woes of life ? The fact is that the reality of the situation is that most of the people are flocked by a big battalion of so called friends, but when the time comes to test the friendship you find not one amidst you. This happens to be the reality of life. At some point of time in your life you might have experienced this reality. The fact also remains that when you have a big group of friends at your command you feel very happy and satisfied and that you start thinking that I will be above to call upon these friends at crisis movements in my life. Unfortunately, the shocking news is that you are not able to get the emotional support from most of this big list of your so called friends. When such is the experience in life you find that at some moment in life you feel depressed, you feel gloomy and that you find that unhappiness is constantly with you. The above situation becomes a common day reality with most of the people. Well, if you are healthy and if you are happy then surely you would not even feel the need and the necessity of depending upon the emotional support of the so called great friendship circle of your. Now no one has time for any one. When most of the people do not have time for their own family members, what to talk of the time to be made available for friends. This is the real paradox of life; hence do realize the reality of the situation and just think ways and vistas, whereby you can experience the miracles of health and happiness in your own life. Believe me, it is possible to do so. Never think it is impossible. I remember the golden words of Walt Disney, the founder of Disneyland, who used to say that if you can dream it you can do it.

My dear friends I want each and every one of you to experience in your own life the magic of Health & Happiness I am sure this little book will help you in achieving for you a wonderful health, and provide you lots of happiness in your day to day life. Medical sciences as you are aware are advancing day in and day out. Still, no capsule is available in the market which will revitalise the happiness in your brain. One would love to have a cap which if worn will start bringing happiness for you. But the fact remains that there is neither a capsule nor a cap which can be used to bring in happiness in you. The best part is that the entire happiness for which you are wondering from place to place lies within you and that it is possible to achieve the miracles of happiness, but only if you were to follow small little pointers contained in this book, which definitely will inspire you to attain your happiness.

One bad happening can spoil the whole barrel of your happiness. Similarly, unhappiness will spread unhappiness amongst the whole group while one happy man will shower the rains of happiness to one and all. You have to be such a person whose presence is going to shower happiness on all those whom you meet in your day to day life.

I strongly believe that investment in happiness is everlasting and ever multiplying investment which will always bring in rich dividends for you. I also strongly feel that if you invest in your own happiness then that would be the best investment ever by you. It was Swami Vivekananda while speaking on Bhakti Yoga in USA said that by being pleasant always and smiling, it takes you nearer to God, nearer than any prayer. How can those minds that are gloomy and dull love? If they talk of love, it is false, they want to hurt others. If you are miserable, try to be happy, try to conquer it..

Normally, our unhappiness and miseries in life comes if we get attached to something, the more we are attached in this materialistic world then more miseries we find in our day to day life. However, it is only happiness with which if we get attached it does not bring any misery. Another strength formula for your happiness is not to get attached to the materialistic world.

However, there is no need to shun them, enjoy your life, enjoy your income, enjoy with your family but do not get attached that is the simple mantra for your blissful happiness. If you want to be attached just get your attachment to God and to nothing else. If there is no happiness in your life, your life may appear to be gloomy so what. Just remember God and it will wash all your unhappiness and gloominess of your life. I strongly believe that in the theory of PRARABDHA. May be my past was not good and I am not happy due to my past prarabdha, hence I must now change my life towards much better vistas so as to build better future Prarabdha for next life.

I am also inspired by the talks given by Swami Vivekananda at different forums. While speaking at Jaffna, Swami Vivekananda said that whatever you think, you will be. If you think you are weak, you will be, if you think yourself as strong, you will be, if you think you are happy, then you will be. Hence, if you want to be happy think that you are really happy and you would be. This is what the Vedas teach us. Never think you are weak, and never think you are unhappy, then happy you will be, Similarly, at London, Swami Vivekananda said, "Life without death and happiness without misery are contradictions and neither can be found alone." He further said, "As soon as a man's horizon increases his horizon of unhappiness increases proportionately."

If you want to be happy, have love with one and all and never have an idea of fear. Always avoid desire, because desire is the father of all miseries. Hence, if you want to be happy do not have too many desires in life. It was Swami Ram Tirth, who said in America that "all fear and anxiety is result of desires, headaches and heartaches are the consequences of desires, so for happiness do away with desires."

If one were to give up entertaining, desires, then surely one will feel exceedingly be happy and would be a fortunate person.

Taittiriya Upanishad belonging to Yajurveda contains a chapter in the Upanishad known as "ANANDAVALLI' which contains higher and higher stages of happiness. One of the verses defining happiness states that human being can achieve the likeness of Brahma (God) through Brahma Vidya or knowledge of Brahma. The happiness at the physical or bodily level is far inferior to the pleasures derived at the mental level. The highest state of happiness is attained through the spirit of inner divinity. The knowledge of the Supreme Brahma is certainly the highest state of happiness.

An interesting paragraph appears in the book Power of Positive Thinking by Norman Vincent Peale. The following is the extract which I am sure will inspire one and all : -

Who decides whether you shall be happy or unhappy? The answer is you do. Someone asked a celebrity "what is the secret of your happiness?" He replied "I haven't any great secret. It's just as plain as the nose of your face. When I get up in the morning, I have two choices either to be happy or to be unhappy and what do you think I do I just choose to be happy and that's all there is to it"

You can be unhappy, if you want to be. It's the easiest thing in the world to accomplish. Just choose unhappiness. Go around telling yourself that things aren't going well, nothing is satisfactory, and you can be quite sure of being unhappy. But say to yourself, "Things are going nicely, life is good, I choose happiness" and you can be quite certain of having your choice. Children are more expert in happiness than adults. God tells us that the way to live in this world is to have a child like heart and mind.

An eleven year girl has this formula for happiness, "Well" she said" I will tell you what it is. My playmates that make me happy, I like them. My school makes me happy. I like to go to school. I like my teachers. I love my sister and brother. I love my father and mother. They take care of me when I am sick and they love me and are good to me."

The happiness habit is developed by simply practicing happy thinking. Make a mental list of happy thoughts and pass them through your mind several times every day.

Keep your heart free from hate, that is, don't let yourself dislike anybody, not the boy in the class who is showing off and getting into trouble, not the teacher who blames you for what you didn't do, Stand up for yourself, straighten out the difficulty but don't brood over it. Don't worry about it. Hate the deed, but not the person, neither dislike anybody; that is if you want to be happy and happy person.

The above statements will inspire the young and the old and would make them enter the kingdom of happiness.

Helen Killer, who said that happiness, cannot come from without. It must come from within. It is not what we see and touch or that which others do for us which makes us happy, it is that which we think and feel and do, first for the other fellow and then for ourselves that really makes us happy. So, if you want to be happy, then be happy and thus enjoy the bliss of life.

2. Vowels of Happiness

The magic of Health & Happiness can be experienced by each and every person on this earth. I strongly feel that if you want to be happy, love one and all and also never have an idea of fear. It is also true that the absence of desire should be your motto if you want to be happy. I remember way back, nearly 110 years ago, Swami Vivekananda while speaking in Los Angeles said that desire is a father of misery. Therefore, said Swami Vivekananda to be happy and have no desire, because desires may bring miseries for you. Swami Vivekananda further went on to say that this world is a place. You are his playmates. Go on and work, without any sorrow and the miseries. If you do so, I feel you will get happiness opined Swami Vivekananda. Well what was said by Swami Vivekananda, a century ago, sill holds good today. From the above thinking of Swami Vivekananda one thing is crystal clear and that is that even a century ago getting happiness was an important item.

Waves from the ocean of Bhakti contain a beautiful quotation which says that — The infinite and eternal happiness cannot be gained through finite and perishable things. That is the reason that young Nachiketa renouncing all forms of enjoyment craved only for Eternal Bliss.

When we talk about miracles of health and happiness, we are forced to believe the fact that money alone cannot buy happiness. I remember the days of John D. Rockfeller, who at that time was the youngest billionaire of USA. But people used to burn his effigies daily and that he was not able to sleep well and also in his middle age he was looking like an old man. So, the fact is that he had money but he had no happiness. One night, he realised that he will not be able to take a single dollar with him. This thought came to him, at one midnight. And this thought alone was responsible for changing his life and he now decided to give, and so was born a great Rockfeller Foundation.

About two year ago, a newspaper report said that elite British Universities have unhappiest students. Really surprising? The newspaper report said that the elite British Universities, in which it was very difficult to get the admission, but unfortunately, even in some of these most prestigious universities of the world, the students studying in these universities were the unhappiest students. Well, this type of news when it is printed it makes one think, well just getting admission in one of the best universities is alone not going to bring happiness for you. The fact remains, neither money nor the high educational qualifications which will produce happiness for you but happiness can still be enjoyed by you, if you take care to preserve your happiness and do not rely upon merely on materialistic world. Deanna Mascle the teacher and freelance writer in the United States said that have you ever wondered where you fall on the happiness scale? Are most people happier or less happy than you are? According to a Scripps Howard Ohio University survey done in the US, 52% of Americans say they are "very happy" with their lives, with 43% reporting they are "fairly happy," 3% said they are 'not too happy" and 2% undecided in Britain. Gallup polls show that only 36% claim they are "very happy" which is down from 52% in 1957. In a very interesting article, the Deanna Mascle further went on to pose a question Namely, can you? Can you imagine possessing the power to spread smiles? You do not need to imagine it because you already possess that power. You simply need to get yourself in the habit of smiling. Smile at your loves ones, smile at your friends. And smile at stranger on the street, and soon you will be making a strong contribution to make the world a happier place. Your happiness is important because you are a significant person, your mood impacts your family and friends, and your happiness affects the world.

The magic of happiness definitely can be felt if you start smiling right now; not merely for your happiness but for providing happiness to one and all human beings whom you meet in your journey in this world.

I also feel that one can experience the magic of happiness, if one were to adopt VRS formula of the reading. This VRS formula for reading is to read spiritual literatures written by Swami Vivekananda, Swami Ram Tirath, and Shivanand (VRS). This will definitely help you to attain more happiness in your life.

The magic of health and happiness can be achieved by you, if you take out quality time and think on the mission and aim of your own life. To answer this small little question you would require an hour but the outcome of correct conclusion can be reached by you only if you think of spending a couple of hours in a day to write and then rewrite your own statement of mission and aim of your life. Once you write down your own mission and aim of life and then do read your mission statement on a regular basis which will provide happiness to you as and when you progress well in the wonderland of achieving your own mission in this life. Hence, while keeping yourself happy & healthy, do take up time to settle down your mission statement and get the magic of happiness experienced by you.

These days' psychosomatic diseases cause a lot of worries and tension to crores of people the world over. However, if one is happy then these psychosomatic diseases can become a thing of the past.

At one point of time in your life you may experience in your own life time when the physicians fail but the spiritual feeling can do miracles for one and all, hence if you want to experience the magic of health, do have faith in spiritual heeling and cure your illnesses, cure your various diseases and goon spreading the message of spiritual heeling to one and all. Please do remember that spiritual heeling is effective and economical and comes to you almost free of cost. The fact also remains that powers of prayer if realised by a person can help him remove his diseases to a great extent and this is mainly because of the faith you may have in the Almighty God and this faith coupled with sincere and dedicated prayers can bring magic in your entire life in the sphere of better health and providing unprecedented happiness all round.

Through faith of spiritual feelings, indirectly you are helping someone to have a spiritual knowledge; spiritual knowledge has been accepted as the highest gift which can be given by a person.

Thinking negativity takes away all your creativity and helps you to enter the zone of unhappiness and unhealthy life and hence if you want to enjoy and experience the magic of health and happiness never ever think of negativity. Start constructing happiness effectively in your own kingdom and experience and let the production of happiness grow in you and thereafter start spreading and distributing the happiness to one and all who comes in your contact.

It is also seen that loneliness can be a cause of being unhealthy and can result into vanishing your happiness. Hence, it time to share your loneliness and get around people either by joining a sports group, going to a club or going to a kitty party or developing of group of like-minded person.

One can also buy happiness. Sounds somewhat strange but the fact is that in realty one can definitely buy happiness and this happiness can be bought by you by spending a small little money in helping the downtrodden and helping the needy and in extending some financial assistance to deserving poor and needy persons. This is the formula of buying happiness for you. This type of happiness remains for pretty very long time.

Over 150 years ago, Leo Tolstoy thought of giving happiness to earth. He first experienced happiness for himself and then he went on to give happiness to the people on the earth. I remember Edward Bob the editor of lady home Journal which was selling nearly two lakhs copies at that time, found himself to be unhappy. He left business and decided to devote his time and money to philanthropy's world for getting to experience happiness. At one time his view was money is king and business is our God. But he changed his own motto and he became firm believer of the fact that the greatest happiness of life is with oneself and money alone cannot buy happiness.

The happiness formula of Wilfred Paterson which is very dear to my heart says that happiness does not come from doing what we like to do but from likening what we have to do.

This happiness formula, I have myself practiced in my real life and I have benefited a lot with this practical formula. I am sure if the readers of this book were to adopt this simple formula on happiness by Wilfred Peterson then surely you will experience the magic of happiness.

I have designed separate vowels for happiness and these vowels for happiness are as under:-

(a) Visible to attachment No, and anger No.
(e) Visible to egolessness.
(i) Introspection in the presence of God.
(o) Visible to oneness to God.
(u) Visible to universal brotherhood.

I feel that if one follows these vowels summary in day

to day life then surely they will be able to have better years to come.

One should always be contented in one's life and that happens to be a single formula for enjoying the magic of happiness in life. Andrew Carnegie was very sad on his death bed at that time he realised the importance of being contended in life.

Dr. Michael Castles, a renowned personality, gave a wonderful formula for happiness and this formula was that you have to be a prisoner of life pressures, hence never pressure in life come between your happiness. Enjoy life as it comes. Slow down when you reach 50 + age. Work, work hard, but don't take too much pressure on your health.

If we walk through the pages of Vedas, we are also able to find happiness formulae through different Vedas some of the happiness formulae as contained in the Vedas should be read again and again.

A serious reader interested to acquire more and more happiness can go through Vedas in greater details so that happiness formulae can be experienced in real life.

Speaking about true happiness, Swami Ram Dass used to say that eternal happiness, the inner life and concentration and meditation on the same will help you to derive true happiness in your own life.

If you want to experience happiness in our own life and experience superior happiness the wonderful happiness then for the real happiness the best formula is, don't give up. It would be worthwhile if you listen to wonderful song with the caption do not give up by Peter Gabrile Kate Bush.

3. Your Kingdom of Joy with Your Happiness

Live in your kingdom of joy like a Lord, but that is possible but only if you keep happiness close to your heart. One such formula for keeping happiness close to your heart is to let goodness remain with you always. Always do remember that your goodness should remain goodness for ever and this one simple formula will be instrumental for your own happiness. My father Shri R.N. Lakhotia has been propagating the theme of goodness at every point of time at every moment in life at every situation. He has not only been suggesting to the people around him to remain good at all the time, but he has been following and practising the precept of goodness to one and to all. Being inspired by his real life example, myself, my wife Sushila and my son Satyapriya we are completely dedicated to the concept of extending our goodness always in all situations and under all circumstances. Believe me this is the reality that if you continue to extend goodness, then happiness always is near to you.

I know sometimes you may feel that it is not easy and simple to extend goodness in a situation where you might have been betrayed by someone or in a situation where you have been cheated by someone or in a situation where some unpleasant happening has happened. But do please remember that for the sake of your own happiness at least it is time now for you to continue to extend goodness at every point of time in your life. Also please accept that the reality of the situation is that only if you extend goodness, then you will remain happy for ever. A large number of illnesses are due to the fact that we are not happy and now that if you want that illness should not come near you, then the answer is always let your goodness prevails over everything else. Change your thinking. Yes, do change your thinking. Accept the miracles of the life which can be achieved by you in the form of a wonderful fountain of happiness near you all the time mainly because you are adopting the concept of extending goodness always in all situations.

The happiness in your own Kingdom of Joy can become reality only when you want it to become. Hence, first you should dream that you want happiness in your wonderful Kingdom of Joy. I recollect the following wonderful lines of a poem written by Swami Satyananda Saraswati which inspires me. Here are these inspiring lines.

> You have to mount a white swan
> Make sure that you're balanced and firm.
> If you sit in the right way
> His feathers will feel warm and comfortable.
> Then fly through the dark night of chidakash.
> Thousands of light years ahead of you
> Is a small light point
> That is what you must fix your mind upon.
> You will cross many oceans of samskaras,
> Mountains of thoughts and valleys of depression.

I feel that the valleys of depression can definitely be conquered by white swans described in the few lines of the poetry by Swami Satyananda Saraswati. One should always aim at bringing happiness in every moment in one's life. I remember an interesting anecdote which was printed in a magazine entitled Aryan Heritage. Here goes the anecdote.

Rajaji was the first Governor General of India, who was a freedom fighter, writer and a great scholar. He was once asked: "Sir! What is the happiest moment in your life?" Rajaji's answer was: "Two hot idles from the hot idly-maker have to be brought. I would soak the idlies with the chillies powder treated with gingelly oil on either side. My tongue should be hot both ways : One because of hot idlies and the other because of red chilli powder. When the tongue is so very hot, a nicely made South Indian filtered Coffee should be brought steaming. The coffee in a stainless steel tumbler should be so hot that I am not able to hold it in my hand. I should use my towel to hold the tumbler I should pour it into my tongue directly in the process two drops of tears should emerge from my eyes and fall! That is the happiest moment in my life."

The Six big Mistakes of a Man as illustrated by Cicero are as under:

1. The illusion that personal gain is made by crushing others.
2. The tendency to worry about things that cannot be changed or rectified.
3. Insisting that a thing is impossible because we cannot accomplish it.
4. Refusing to set aside trivial preferences.
5. Neglecting development and refinement of the mind, and not acquiring the habit of self-analysis.
6. Attempting to compel others to believe and live just like we do.

Thus, to correct above mentioned six mistakes the simple formula is to be happy always at every point of time in life. Sometimes some real life stories which one may read here and there may inspire every human person to get some small little pinch of happiness by reading the real life drama stories. One such story which I read the other day and which is dear to me was printed in the magazine Aryan Heritage under the caption "A Glass of Milk." This story after you read will provide happiness to you and I feel that the same type of happiness I may derive some day as is contained in this anecdote. Here goes the anecdote.

One day, a poor boy by the name of Howard Kelly was selling clothing door to door to pay for his education. He realised that he only had ten cents left in his pocket. He was hungry and so decided to ask for some food at the next house that he came to.

In the meantime, he lost his hunger when a beautiful young woman opened the door. Instead of a meal, he asked her for a glass of water.

She saw that he was very hungry so instead brought him a huge glass of milk. He drank it very slowly and then asked, "How much do I owe you?"

"You do not owe me anything at all," she replied, "My mother taught us never to accept anything for doing someone a kindness."

He replied, "Then I thank you from the bottom of my heart."

When Howard Kelly left the house, as well as feeling stronger physically, he sensed a return of his faith in the Lord which he had nearly abandoned.

Years later, the same young woman fell gravely ill. The local doctors were mystified, so they sent her to the big city where they knew that the specialists would be able to diagnose this rare sickness.

Doctor Howard Kelly was called as a consultant. When he read the name of the city where she lived, a memory burned brightly in his eyes. He got up and went to her room. As he entered her room, he immediately recognised her. He returned to the consultation room, determined to do his best to save her life. From that day on, he paid special attention to this case. After a long battle, the war was finally won.

Doctor Kelly left instructions that the bill should be sent to him for authorisation. He looked it over, wrote something in the margin and sent it to her room. She thought that when she opened the envelope she would find an invoice that would take the rest of her life to pay in full. But, when she finally opened it, something caught her attention in the margin of the invoice. She read these words, "Paid in full for a glass of milk : Doctor Howard Kelly."

Swami Sivananda used to say that one should practise silent meditation, It is through this silent meditation that you start really enjoying the Kingdom of Joy, your own Kingdom and the answer is only through deriving happiness and happiness alone.

Once a wonderful Vedantic thought was published in the Vedanta Kesari which really inspired me and I am sure this thought will also inspire a lot of my readers.

It was mentioned in this thought that:

To him who has nothing in the universe, the Lord comes. Cut the bondage of all worldly affections; go beyond all care as to what becomes of you... there is no time to seek money, or name, or fame, no time to think of anything but God; then will come into our hearts that infinite, wonderful bliss of love.

Sometimes a question may also arise as to what you believe in. The other day I read a small write up about what I believe. I read again and again and finally I was convinced that what was printed was as if relating to me and me alone. Please try for yourself the underlined passage dealing with the concept I believe and may be you will find that what is written in the foregoing paragraph is actually relevant for you in spirit and in action.

I BELIEVE

I believe – that we don't have to change friends if we understand that friends change.

I believe - that no matter how good a friend is, they're going to hurt you every once in a while and you must forgive them for that.

I believe - that true friendship continues to grow, even over the longest distance. Same goes for true love.

I believe – that you can do something in an instant that will give you heartache for life.

I believe - that it's taking me a long time to become the person I want to be.

I believe - that you should always leave loved ones with loving words. It may be the last time you see them.

I believe - that you can keep going long after you can't.

I believe - that we are responsible for what we do, no matter how we feel.

I believe - that either you control your attitude or it controls you.

I believe - that regardless of how hot and steamy a relationship is at first, the passion fades and there had better be something else to take its place.

I believe - that heroes are the people who do what has to be done when it needs to be done, regardless of the consequences.

I believe - that money is a lousy way of keeping score.

I believe - that my best friend and I can do anything or nothing and have the best time.

I believe- that sometimes the people you expect to kick you when you're down, will be the ones to help you get back up.

I believe- that sometimes when I'm angry I have the right to be angry, but that doesn't give me the right to be cruel.

I believe - that just because someone doesn't love you the way you want them to doesn't mean they don't love you with all they have.

I believe - that maturity has more to do with what types of experiences you've had and what you've learned from them and less to do with how many birthdays you've celebrated.

I believe - that it isn't always enough to be forgiven by others. Sometimes you have to learn to forgive yourself.

I believe - that no matter how hard your heart is broken the world doesn't stop for your grief.

I believe - that our background and circumstances may have influenced who we are, but we are responsible for who we become.

I believe - that just because two people argue, it doesn't mean they don't love each other and just because they don't argue, it doesn't mean they do.

I believe - that you shouldn't be so eager to find out a secret. It could change your life forever.

I believe - that two people can look at the exact same thing and see something totally different.

I believe - that your life can be changed in a matter of hours by people who don't even know you.

I believe - that even when you think you have no more to give, when a friend cries out to you, you will find the strength to help.

I believe - that credentials on the wall do not make you a decent human being.

I believe – that the people you care about most in life

are taken from you too soon.

Dear Reader, just remember that the Kingdom of Joy is your own Kingdom and as the Kingdom is yours, the joy is also yours. But to achieve the real joy the answer is to find happiness. Always think of finding happiness in a small little activity which you carry out in the whole day. Do remember also that even a small little action or on activity can provide you a real joy which can become the joy in your Kingdom and bring happiness to you. The ever last happiness, that should be the your goal.

4. Out from Anger Acid for Your Own Health and Happiness

We are all afraid of acid but the word acid which can cause the maximum loss and disadvantage is the "Anger Acid" which I call it AA. This Anger Acid is such that if it comes into action, then it has got the capacity to take away your entire gamut of happiness. Hence, always keep away from the sprinkles of this Anger Acid. Never be angry, this in brief should be your sole motto of life. Let this be the real motto of life and then you find that you are a relaxed person and you are a happy person. You must have all read about one famous quotation which said that anger is an acid which does more harm to the person with whom it is stored than the person on whom it is poured. This is the reality of the situation. Read this quotation again and again and then you find that you are able to realise the importance and the gravity of this anger acid. Hence, never be angry at any time on any situation. It is a fact that you can always justify your anger. Your justification may really be justification with the reasoning but the fact remains that if we are angry, we are unhappy. Therefore, always keep the anger acid away. Otherwise, it is going to affect your health and happiness. The anger acid is one of the worst acid to cause irreparable damage to your health. Your emotion gets disturbed when you are angry. Your outer body may not experience any change but the inner body of yours experiences great humiliation, great depression, great uneasiness only due to this anger acid of yours. Hence, it is time for you now to avoid this anger acid at all situation in all circumstances.

One of the ways to avoid the anger acid is never to argue and mainly never argue just for your own bliss and happiness.

Never argue. Never enter into an argument. Why do you want to win an argument ? It offers you no tangible benefit. It will only inflate your ego, wound the other man and lead to friction between friends.

Let the other man hold his opinion. There are incorrigible idiols in this world who can never be converted, who can never be made to see sense. Do not waste your time and breath on them. You will only suffer exhaustion and earn enmity. These lines I found in one quotation by some famous writer.

The fragrance of anger acid and its sprinkling causes not merely damage to health but also takes away your happiness in entirety. Hence, always keep away from this bottle of anger acid. In the initial situation you may find it difficult to control your anger but the fact is the more and more you realise the necessity and the importance and the utility of your health and your happiness, then surely you will make your anger as a thing of the past and would never ever let anger acid approach you in any situation. The other day I read a small write up about ABC of happiness. Well here is the ABC of happiness which after reading will inspire you to be happy.

A	Aspire to reach your potential.
B	Be a positive thinker of life.
C	Create a good life.
D	Dream about what you might become.
E	Encourage self responsibility.
F	Fair dealing always pays in your life.
G	Give honest and sincere appreciations.
H	Have what people value.
I	Imagine great things.

J	Joyfully live each day.
K	Keep interest in your job.
L	Learn to listen.
M	Maintain an action oriented environment.
N	Neatness will keep diseases away.
O	Organise for time bound plan.
P	Plan your work and work your plan.
Q	Question most things.
R	Remember after sorrow comes happiness.
S	Smile often speak softly.
T	Take time to serve humanity.
U	Understand people and yourself.
V	View the minds of your people as resources.
W	Wipe out your weakness.
X	X-ray and carefully examine your problems.
Y	Yearn to improve.
Z	Zestfully pursue happiness.

It is suggested that one should avoid the seeds of anger acid and let come in of the seeds of gratitude in life. The seeds of gratitude if they enter your mind and body, they will surely help you in realising your own better health and better happiness. I remember the actual life story of Vidyasagar. This story is with reference to gratitude in life. Here is the actual life story of Vidyasagar which is printed hereunder which I read couple of years ago and the memory of the actual life story relating to gratitude is ever fresh in my memory.

Vidyasagar, the noble teacher, met in Burdwan a poor thin boy at the time of the famine of 1865. That boy begged for a paisa. There was a bright look on his pale face.

"Suppose that I give you four paise," said Vidyasagar.

"Do not jest, sir,"

"I am not jesting. What would you do with four paise?"

"Buy something to eat with two, and I shall give two paise to my mother."

"And suppose I give you two annas?"

The boy turned away but Vidyasagar caught him by his arms.

"Tell me."

Tears ran down the boy's cheeks.

I shall buy rice with four paise, and I shall give the rest to mother."

"And what about four annas?"

"I shall use two annas for two days' food, and I shall buy mangoes worth two annas. I shall sell those mangoes for four annas, and so I shall go on trading, and thus keep my mother and myself alive."

Vidyasagar gave him a rupee, and the lad ran sway, in sheer joy.

Two years later, Vidyasagar again visited Burdwan: A stout, strong youth stepped out from a shop and saluted.

"Please, sir, may I ask you to take a seat in my shop?"

"I do not know you."

With tears in his eyes, the lad told how Vidyasagar had helped him two years ago and he was now a man with a nice little business. Vidyasagar blessed the youth, and sat awhile in the shop.

How charming it is to think of Vidyasagar sitting in the dealer's shop and chatting as a friend! The two souls were knit together by the bond of gratitude.

If you are not able to control yourself from the anger acid in your mind and your body, then start reading a small little spiritual write-up, which will help you in the process of your getting away from anger acid. One such small write-up, which I hope you would love to read is by the Grand Master Choa Kok Sui of the Pranic Healing. This is the great invocation by the said Grand Master, Choa Kok Sui:

> From the point of Light within the Mind of God,
> Let Light stream forth into the minds of men,
> Let Light descend on Earth.
> From the point of Love within the Heart of God,
> Let Love stream forth into the hearts of men,
> May God return to Earth.
> From the centre where the Will of God is known,
> Let purpose guide the little wills of men,
> The purpose which the Masters know and serve.
> From the centre which we call the race of men,
> Let the Plan of Love and Light work out,
> and may it seal the door where evil dwells.
> Let Light and Love and Power,
> Restore the Plan on Earth.

If you are or you were till recently associated with anger acid, then it is time now to throw away this model of anger acid and start a fresh day just by looking into the various negative effects which anger acid may bring in your life and then, you find better health and better happiness for you at all times.

5. Fear Psychosis

Fear psychosis can eat into your health and happiness. The fact is that we all human-beings in the whole world are interested to have robust health and exceptional happiness in their day-to-day life. Sometimes, this question crops up in our mind and we may not be able to find the answer and this question is that everyone wants good health and good happiness, how come it will become a realty for everyone. Well, my research and interaction with lakhs of wonderful and fine persons all the world over has given me one conclusion that fear psychosis is one of the very important features to ruin your health and to take away your happiness. When a person gets worried and tense just because of some fear psychosis, then his metabolic equation of the body goes wrong and immediately he finds himself in a dark corner where day by day his health gets deteriorated and happiness becomes a thing of past. Hence, in these circumstances, one very important point is never to have fear, especially for all that which has not happened. Please keep in mind one important point and that is if you are fearful, your brain will stop working in creation of creative solutions for you. Hence, never ever think about those things which have not happened and who knows you may be unnecessarily worrying about the same. Stop immediately brooding over all those items which have not happened and start thinking and acting only with a positive note in your mind. I remember one of my friend received a notice from the Income Tax Department. By just seeing a letter from the Tax Department, he went into the fear zone. Fear psychosis was on its top end. That evening, he was not able to take his dinner in a happy mood. His anguish could be reflected in his dealing with the staff and the family members. He thought that he may be ruined as a result of outcome of that Tax notice. But unfortunately, the fact was that he had not read the contents of that notice. When he met me next day, he explained that last night was a very tough time. He was unable to sleep and whole night he was dreaming and thinking about the Income Tax notice. He brought the notice to me. He did not even read it. When I glanced through the notice, a big laughter was reflected on my face. He was surprised and immediately in anger he felt that I am having a tough tension and a great fear because of this notice from the Tax Department, but you are feeling so happy and you are laughing by seeing the notice. I told him please be calm and quiet and now we start reading the contents of the notice. The notice just said that Tax Department wanted a copy of the tax challan in case the payment has been made. Nothing more was contained in this notice.

When my friend read the notice with me in togetherness he thought that what a big fool he was because he was only having a great fear psychosis as a result of receiving the notice from the Tax Department. My dear friends, at any point of time, even if there is tension, even if there is calamity, take it easy. In majority of the cases the chances are that your problem will be solved without any hassles and tension but just to worry for all that which has not happened is not going to bring any major relief or benefit to you. Similarly, I found in my career as a Tax Consultant for the last over 40 years that lot of tax payers in India are worried about Income Tax raids and survey. At the back of their mind, there is a fear that by chance if Income Tax raid takes place what is going to happen and just a thought about expected Income Tax raid on their premises made their face gloomy and unhappiness can be seen on their face round the clock. Their digestive system gets disturbed due to worry and tension because of the proposed and expected Income Tax raid taking place on their family premises. Well, to such persons, my advise always has been that they should take care but never to worry for all that which has not happened. When we go at any hospital, we are able to see dreadful eyes and the faces not of the patients but of the relatives of the patients coming to the hospital.

We can understand that the patient face shows gloomy face because he is suffering, he is in pain, he is having the problem, he is having disease and he is having difficulty, but there should be no gloomy face of the relatives and the attendants of the patient. But generally, the fact remains that in majority of cases for the relatives we find that their faces are full of fear psychosis as soon as they enter the hospital entrance. Due to this fear psychosis, the relatives and the attendants of the patient loose their own happiness, their own health and they lack in proper medical care of their relative. Hence, if you want peace and you want happiness and your want robust health, then always say a BIG GOOD BYE to the fear psychosis in your brain.

6. Adopt WAP Formula for Your Health and Happiness

I have been myself practicing WAP formula to overcome my own health and happiness problems. I can now say with conviction that WAP is the real golden mantra to avoid all your tensions, worries and problems and to bring better health for you coupled with unprecedented happiness in your day to day life. Well, this is possible because of this WAP formula. The question that would now be coming in the minds of the readers is after all what is this WAP formula then adopt this formula with success. Well, this WAP formula designed by me is known as work action plan. If you want to achieve health and happiness for you and for all the members of the family. At any point of time when you find your family member or you or a relative or a friend is suffering from some health disorder and you could see the frightened faces of the family as a result of this health problem at that point of time for better health and to achieve this miracle of health, one should completely concentrate on this WAP programme viz the work action plan should start instantly and immediately to cater to the required better medical facility to be provided to this relative or family member of yours. If you adopt this WAP formula in a situation when someone in the family is not well instantly you will immediately stop talking negative and would just concentrate only on action plan for providing the best medical facility to such person. Yes, for better health, WAP is the only answer even in crisis, even in turmoil times, even when a great big problem has taken place relating to health disorder of some of your family member or your own health disorder is in the offing. At that point of time, just concentrate, meditate, and think of best action plan to be adopted and that alone is the best answer for your health and to bring happiness for you in the family under the given circumstance.

I remember, when my mother was suffering from cancer, my son Satyapriya very extensively undertook this WAP programme in real life situation instead of worrying 24x7 about cancer problem of my mother. He was actively engaged in doing research about the medical problem and talking to the Doctors in various hospitals and then coming to conclusive solution for providing medical facility. At that point of time, he was also very active in adopting WAP formula for coming to positive conclusion relating to medical aspect connected with the medical treatment of my late mother. When I sit down sometime thinking about the past, I find that if Satyapriya would not have adopted the real life WAP programme then life would have still been troublesome, still more torturous because in the absence of WAP formula, how can one can take care of the health problems of a family member. It was just WAP formula which my son transplanted later in real life tension situation and this WAP programme brought wonderful results for us. Just imagine, instead of adopting this WAP programme if we all family members including my son would just sit and worry then there would be health disaster in family and our happiness in any case would be out of gear and the health of the family members would not bring any positive results and at that point of time, when there is crisis in the family when there is health crisis, the best answer is to adopt is only this WAP formula — the work action plan. This WAP formula alone will bring miracle to the health of your own or the health of your family. Similarly, when it comes to happiness, you may find at one point of time or at many points of time or at every point of time in real life situation when you are unhappy. Why are you unhappy is not the question, but the question is how to become happy in adverse situation and the simple answer is that all those situations which have made you unhappy think on them and then adopt WAP programme viz work action plan to achieve your happiness and if WAP programme is implemented to retain or to gain your happiness surely it would do wonder and bring happiness in your life cycle.

Not merely you should adopt WAP programme but once you find the wonderful results of WAP prgramme becoming a realty in your own life then at that point of time I would suggest you to place introduce WAP programme to your friends and relatives and let them also experience the realty of life of fighting with health problems and fighting with unhappiness issues through WAP programme. Viz. One Action Plan Programme.

7. Fast and Not Feast: the Mantra for Your Health

When you make materialistic progress in your life then suddenly you find many things change in your life. Your life style also changes. You're dressing sense changes too. You're shopping habits change and so changes your food habits. Generally, it is seen that when a person makes materialistic progress in his life and suddenly one fine day he finds lot of money under his command then surely he thinks of spending a lot on eating habits too. Feast and feast becomes the only world for such persons. These persons now think that because of abundance of money power at that their and command, they will be able to eat what they like and at that point of time when they like. Suddenly, with the influx of increase in the standard of eating habits due to big money power, the sudden fall is simultaneously reflected in the health and well being of a person.

It is suggested that for your own health, please do not lay emphasis on feast but let lay your emphasis on fast. If you want to be healthy then take time to fast for 24 hours at least once in a month. If we adopt the habits of fasting then surely it becomes very good for the up keep of our health, because due to fasting we are able to keep our body in the natural way. We all appreciate and understand the importance of rest and relaxation, hence think of providing such rests and relaxation to your body at least once in a month. If you are ready to follow this path of fasting at least once a month then surely you will be able to have better health in comparison to your other friends and relatives. However, the best combination for health seeker is to adopt the concept of fasting at least once a week. The ideal answer is to fix a particular day of the week and fast on that day. The problem of obesity can never disturb you if you adopt the concept of fasting on a regular basis. The day when you are fasting, try to live only on liquid diet. Some time people think that we cannot adopt fasting because it will make us weak and thin and we will not be able to carry out our regular activities on that day. Well, this is not correct. Merely fasting for just one day, your capacity to work or your strength will increase but will not decrease. You can try this formula for your own health and happiness.

Myself and my father we have been fasting for half day once in a week for the last over 40 years and we find it a very good stimulus for our health. Hence, if you are interested to take care of your health and you want to preserve better health for you even in old days, then it is time for you now to concentrate on the theme of fast and not feast at least once a month. Gradually, when you yourself experience the benefits of fasting at that point of time, try to extend your fasting to once a week.

For achieving best result on the day of fasting, it is recommended that the day when you are fasting on that day try to keep your active life at least at a slow pace and try to concentrate on reading spiritual literature on think on relaxing for some time. Once you fast for 24 hours, you will find that your energy level is great and the toxin elements from your body are removed, you will feel yourself very light and you feel very happy too. Hence, develop for yourself this habit of fasting and once you have developed the habit of fasting and you have experienced the fantastic advantages of the fasting, thereafter, start extending this magic formula for healing to your family members. On the day of your fast just take liquid diet and stay on soup, fruits and vegetables. I have found that on the day of fast, taking just one variety of food the whole day helps you a lot. Similarly, while talking about vegetables, take boiled vegetables without putting any salt etc., and then you find that your body becomes light. Although, you would like to control obesity also for that fasting is a good example of keeping healthy.

The fantastic advantages of fasting results into curing obesity also. However, keeping obesity under control becomes a reality when you are fasting for a long time. If you want to adopt complete sure success formula of reducing weight then regular fasting for few days every half year, will bring very good results for you. However, if you want to undertake fasting programme of more than one day, may be say 5 days to 15 days, then such fasting activities should be undertaken only under the expert guidance of a doctor or a Naturopath. I have seen hundreds of person being cured just by this magic formula of fasting, hence if you want to be healthy and that also without medicines then you should adopt this magic formula of fasting which will provide energy and strength to you and burn your problems related to health.

Hence, fast and not feast should be the Mantra to be adopted by you for your own health and well-being. Just remember, in fasting you find a wonderful spiritual formula of restoring your health without any extra arrangements to be done.

Instead of fasting, if you resort to the formula of feasting and think every time is a feast time then definitely your health will be out of order. A person only sticking to the formula of feast may not find any problem in the initial stages especially due to the young age but with the advancement of age the feast would result into problems for you.

You can lay emphasis even on feast programme for you but not too such feasting which is not good for your health, hence, always be attach to the mantra of fast and not feast for your own robust vibrant health.

The Central Council for Research in Yoga and Naturopathy describes fasting is an important modality in the natural methods of health preservation. For fasting, mental preparedness is an essential precondition. Fasting for just one or two days, can be administered to any individual. Prolong fasting should be done only under supervision of competent Naturopath.

Naturopathy believes that fasting is a process of giving rest to the digestive system. During this process, the vital energy which digests the food is wholly engaged in the eliminative process. This is the object of fasting too. Fasting is an excellent treatment for removing the disorders of mind and body. Fasting is advised in treating the disorders like Indigestion, Constipation, Gas, and Digestive disorders, Bronchial Asthma, Obesity, High Blood Pressure and Gout etc.

8. Getting Cured without the Medicines: Nature Cure Way

Every person who is ill is surely interested to be relieved from all the pains and diseases which are affecting him. Whenever a person is ill he just resorts to going on a regular basis to his Doctor, having consultations with the Doctor and then straight going to the medical shop, to buy the medicines and coming home and start taking medicines. This is the cycle of life for those people who are ill and are having a bad health. In spite of following this circle for health progress, when a person finds that his health is not recovering in spite of meeting a Doctor and taking the medicines then starts another big road therein to met more and more doctors and medical consultants for cure of your ailments and diseases. It is a fact that when a person is ill, he is not able to take advantage of enjoying the life; hence health should be the concern of each and every one and should be on the top most agenda of everyone especially when they want to enjoy their life in this world.

I strongly believe that adopting the Nature cure way comes very handy for curing most of your health related disorders and that too without medicines. The nature cure concept is such a concept whereby without any side effects it is able to cure almost all your health related problems. I myself am a strong believer of the principles of nature cure concept of health treatment. I have also experienced the magic of Nature Cure treatment. I remember way back nearly 30 years ago when my father met a Dr. and the Dr. advised him of some heart disorder and immediately a big list was prepared of the action plan. Suddenly, this type of message when comes from the Dr. the family gets frightened and disturbed, but as we great have faith in the nature cure concept my father just adopted the nature cure ways of removing body disorders.

I am happy to place on record that in the last 30 years he has never had any health related major problems and disorders and the credit goes only to the natural way of living and adopting the nature cure principles in day to day life.

The fact remains that the Government of India also is realising the importance of nature cure system of treatment and hence the Government of India Ministry of Health and Family Welfare, Department of Ayush, has formed an organisation known by the name of Central Council for Research in Yoga and Naturopathy. This organisation is very actively engaged in brining home for the benefit of the citizens of India, the great big advantages of naturopathy. Before coming to the principles of nature cure, it will be worthwhile for the readers to understand the main principles of naturopathy or the nature cure treatments, which have been very wonderfully explained by the Central Council for Research in Yoga and Naturopathy. Here are the main principles of naturopathy, which are as under:

1. All diseases, their cause and their treatment are one. Except for traumatic and environmental conditions, the cause of all diseases is one i.e. accumulation of morbid matter in the body and their elimination from the body is the treatment.
2. The primary cause of disease is not bacteria. Bacteria and virus invades and survives in the body only after the accumulation of morbid matter when a favourable atmosphere for their growth is established in the body. Basic cause is morbid matter, not the bacteria or virus. They are secondary cause.

3. Acute diseases are our friends, not the enemy. Chronic diseases are the outcome of wrong treatment and suppression of the acute diseases.
4. Nature is the greatest healer. Body has a capacity to prevent itself from diseases and regain health if fallen ill.
5. In naturopathy patient is treated and not the disease.
6. In Naturopathy diagnosis is easily possible. Ostentation does not require. Long waiting for diagnosis does not require for treatment.
7. Patient suffering from chronic ailments are also treated successfully in comparatively less time in Naturopathy.
8. Suppressed diseases can also be cured by Naturopathy.
9. Nature Cure takes into consideration physical, mental, social (moral) and spiritual all four aspects altogether.
10. Nature Cure treats body as a whole instead of giving treatment to specific condition.
11. Naturopathy does not use medicines. According to Naturopathy "Food is Medicine."
12. According to Gandhiji, "**Rama Nama is the best Natural Treatment,**" whereby he means doing prayer according to one's faith should be an important part of treatment.

The principles of natural living and adopting the concept of Nature Cure may be new to the India but this concept of nature cure has been followed by western countries since long time. In India for the last more than hundred years, we are able to see the progress of nature cure. A famous book by Louis Kuhne, titled "New Types of Healing," should be read by all those persons who are interested in adopting the Nature Cure ways for health treatment. Our father of nation, I mean, Mahatma Gandhi himself used to believe in these great principles of naturopathy and their cure. Gandhiji was influenced by the book "Return to Nature" written by Adolf Just. If you have faith in nature cure then you may also try to read this book which will help you and will inspire you to follow the nature cure ways of health treatments. After reading the above book, Gandhiji, himself started practicing nature cure treatment for himself and he wrote several articles and books on naturopathy. Earlier nature cure movement which was started long back in Germany and other western countries of the world was known as "Water Cure Movement" because through water cure, a number of health ailments were being cured. Before adopting nature cure as a part of your health cure programme, it may be worthwhile to understand the definition of naturopathy.

Nature Cure or Naturopathy is a system of man building in harmony with constructive principles of Nature on physical, mental, moral and spiritual planes of living. It has great health promotive, disease preventive and curative as well as restorative potential.

Those adopting nature cure principles would find that different modalities are available for curing the diseases under the naturopathy or nature cure way of curing the diseases. The first and the most important principle of nature cure is to change the living habits of the people and that system the nature cure teaches the healthy living style which automatically helps in the progress of gaining a healthy body. Nature cure deals with different modalities to cure the diseases. Some of the important modalities followed under the nature cure system of treatments are, diet therapy, fasting therapy, the mud therapy, the hydro therapy, the massage therapy, the chromo therapy, the air therapy etc. One or more of these modalities help in the process of curing the ailments.

Another important question that crops up in the mind of the readers, as to what are the appellations and diseases which are available through naturopathy. Well, the Central Council for Research in Yoga & Naturopathy (CCRYN) has been trying to verify the efficacy of Naturopathy system in curative and preventive aspects of various diseases by launching research oriented programmes. Based on the research studies under CCRYN projects, the following diseases have been found to be amenable through Naturopathy treatment:

- Anemia
- Allergic Skin Diseases
- Chronic Non-Healing Ulcers
- Colitis
- Diarrhea
- Diabetes Mellitus
- Facial Paralysis
- Gastritis
- Hemiplegia
- Hypertension
- Jaundice
- Leprosy
- Obesity
- Poliomyelitis
- Psoriasis
- Psychosomatic Disorders
- Rheumatoid Arthritis Amoebiasis
- Anxiety
- Cervical Spondylosis

- Cirrhosis of Liver
- Constipation
- Dysentery
- Eczema
- Flatulence
- Gout
- Hypertension
- Hyperacidity
- Leucorrhoea
- Neurosis
- Osteoarthritis
- Peptic Ulcer
- Scabies
- Splenomegaly
- Sciatica

Now, after reading the above mentioned details of nature cure I am sure you will be tempted to adopt the Nature Cure Concept of treatment. In case you require some more details about nature cure then you may contact The Director, Central Council for Research in Yoga & Naturopathy, 61-65, Institutional Area, Janakpuri, New Delhi – 110058. Their website is www.ccryn.org and their e-mail address is ccryn.goi@gmail.com; If you benefit from Nature Cure treatment then do write to the author giving your own practical example.

9. Be Vegetarian for Your Robust Health

If you are vegetarian, you are very likely to have robust health, now and for ever, hence, be vegetarian to enjoy best health for you and for your friends. It has been noticed that persons who are vegetarian generally do not suffer from obesity. Similarly, many dreadful diseases do not easily come close to all those persons who are vegetarian and have developed then habit of consuming only vegetarian food, besides this the nutrient diet is very, very good for health and this is not what I recommend, but this is the fact statement as per World Heath Organisation (WHO). This has also received the approval by the Government of India through Health Bulletin No. 23 and is based on the — some of the contents of protein carbohydrates, essential minerals, (with Iron and Omega-2) and calories in some items of food are given below:-

Table 9-I: Vital Components of Various Foods

Item of Food (per 100 gms)	Protein	Essential Minerals	Carbohydrates	Calories
Vegetarian Foods				
Pulses	24.0	3.6	56.6	334
Soya Beans	43.2	4.6 2.3	20.9	432
Ground Nut	31.5	6.8	19.3	549
Milk Power	38.3	1.9	51.0	357
Non Vegetarian Foods				
Egg	13.3	22.6	1.9 0.8	173
Fish	22.6	18.5	1.3	91
Mutton	18.5			194

Miracles of Health and Happiness

My father, Shri RN Lakhotia, who is also the President of Vegetarian Congress of Delhi, believes that for good health a balanced diet of a person — whether a vegetarian or a non-vegetarian — must include:

(a) carbohydrates;

(b) proteins;

(c) vitamins; and

(d) essential minerals

in his or diet.

Some of the top important Indian personalities, who have been vegetarian, are Ram, Krishna, Gautam Buddha, Mahavira, Thiruvalluvar, Sant Gyaneshwar, Tuka Ram, Nanak, Tulsi Das, Kabir, Meera Bai, Swami Dayanand, Mahatma Gandhi, Gama Pahalwan, Sardar Patel, Dr. Rajendra Prasad, Dr. Radhakrishnan, Dr. Hedgewar, Lal Bahadur Shastri, Abdul Kalam, Amitabh Bachchan.

Vegetarianism is good for health and also been appreciated by the top celebrities in the whole world. Aristotle, Pluto, Socrates, Pythagorus, Shakespeare, Wordsworth, Leo Tolstoy, George Bernard Shaw, Newton, Benjamin Franklin, Darwin, Churchill, Einstein, Martina Navratilova, Madonna, etc. have been vegetarian of their own choice.

My father, Shri R.N. Lakhotia, is constantly spreading the massage of vegetarianism for good health through lot of seminars, which he conducts free at different locations. He has also been delivering talks on vegetarianism at large number of public and private schools.

He is of the view that world famous PETA working for the ethical treatment of animals says that 1 million persons in US alone are turning towards vegetarian diet every year and about 1, 70,00,000 persons in US have now become vegetarians. Sir Paul McCartney, Michael Jackson, Richard

Gere, Pamela Anderson and others had already become vegetarian.

If you have any doubt or clarification you want to see on vegetarianism then please be free to contact Shri R.N. Lakhotia, on 09811025800 and seek for yourself guidance on Vegetarianism and the importance of vegetarianism for your robust health.

10. Gita Saar: the Depression Remover

Believe me when I say that daily if you recite Geeta Saar on regular basis then it is possible to remove your depression. Here is the English Geeta Saar translated by me which if recited on a regular basis will help you in overcoming depression and anxiety. Well, here it is:

- ❖ Why do you worry unnecessarily? From whom do you unnecessarily fear? Who can kill you? Soul (atma) is never born nor does it die.

- ❖ Whatever has happened is good, whatever is going to happen is also good, whatever will happen will also be good. Don't worry about the past. Don't worry about the future and the present is going on.

- ❖ What have you lost that you are weeping. What did you bring that you lost. What did you produce that is perished. You did not bring anything; whatever you have taken you have taken from here. Whatever you have given you have given here. Whatever you have taken you have taken from god and whatever you have given you have given Him. You came with empty hands and with empty hands you will go. Whatever is your's today was belonging to someone yesterday and will be of someone else day after tomorrow. Thinking that this is yours you are becoming happy and this happiness alone is the cause of your miseries and unhappiness.

- ❖ Change is the law of the world. What you think as death that is life. In one second you become the owner of crores of rupees and in another second you just become bankrupt. Yours and mine, big and small, remove these thoughts from your mind and then you will find that everything is yours and you are of everybody.

- ❖ This body is not yours nor you are of the body. This life, water, air, earth are all made of the sky and will get merged with it but Atma is fixed, then what you are. You should surrender yourself to God. This is the most important refuge. One who understands this refuge to God, he is permanently freed from the clutches of fear, worries and sadness.
- ❖ Whatever you are doing you offer it to God and continue your activity. Just by this your life will always be happy and you will enjoy the bliss of your life.

(READ "GEETA SAAR" THRICE A DAY – AVOID DEPRESSION)

11. Happiness from MT: an Experience

The other day, after visiting a construction site, where real state development activities were going on, in respect of residential housing project coming up of my friend at Jangpura, New Delhi, I noticed a sign board with the caption "Missionaries of Charity." Accompanying me was my friend, Vinod, who was the key person behind the construction activities. As soon as I saw the sign board I asked my driver to turn to the right side of the sign board and in next two minutes we were outside a small building at the dead end of the road and this was the building of Missionaries of Charity. It is well known fact that Missionaries of Charity are extending philanthropist activities in different part of India for the less fortunate people of our society. This organisation was founded by Mother Teresa. Hence, I thought, let me just peep inside and find out what type of activities are going on. Just when we landed at the gate of the building, we could see the walls of happiness and the walls of peace which we enjoyed. We just went inside the building and asked for someone who can help us to let us know what activities are going on in the centre so that we could extend some help and assistance. Although, visit to this place was not at all in our agenda for the day's work, but just by seeing the ply card of Missionaries of Charity my car turned from left to right more particularly because of the fact that I have been watching the activities of Mother Teresa, more than last 35 years. While we were in Calcutta, I used to visit Mother Teresa's Centre on my way to Income Tax office. I was working as a Tax Consultant in Calcutta, about 30-35 years, ago and just across the Income Tax Office was situated the International Headquarters of Missionaries of

Charity founded by Mother Teresa. I still remember the warm love and affection with which Mother Teresa welcomed me in her office when I first met her, thereafter small little charities we were giving to the said organisation. I still remember, the day when Mother Teresa called me in her office and asked me to help some children to get a job. I also remember to have visited the vocational centres run by Mother Teresa in Calcutta and whatever I could do, I extended the help of providing service to the children taking these vocational courses. Whenever I talk, whenever I think and whenever I remember these activities, I start feeling happy. The memories of my foreign travels or other occasions may not be that bright even today after the laps of long time but the memories of my quality time spent in the presence of Mother Teresa are still fresh in my memories lanes. I also remember that day when for the first time, when I had met Mother Teresa on 16 Oct 1979 in the big hall of the Raj Bhawan, Calcutta, and I asked Mother Teresa for an autograph with a massage. On my visiting card she wrote "Love others, as God loves you, God bless you - Mother Teresa." The simplicity with which Mother Teresa was working for the welfare of the humanity is fresh in my memory lanes even today and I have no hesitation to say that whenever I visit or I even think about the fine moments spent by me in the company of Mother Teresa I become happy and happy. Now this time, I was visiting the Missionaries of Charity, Jeevan Jyoti Home at Jangpura, New Delhi. Although, me and my friend, Vinod had another appointment in connection with the business meeting but on my insisting Vinod readily agreed and now we entered the Jeevan Jyoti Home. Before one of the sisters could come to met us when we set down in the drawing room in the Jeevan Jyoti Home, we found happiness and peace. It appeared as if happiness and peace was filled in every corner of the room. Well, we could not see happiness, joy and bliss with our necked eyes but frankly speaking we could experience it, while we were waiting in the room. Five minutes later, one of the sisters came to meet us and after giving our introduction to her I told her that we would just like to have a visit at this home of yours and would like to know what you are doing and how help we can help. In next two minutes we were on the first floor of the building and we could see very young orphan children being cared by the sisters of JJH . Our heart was filled with happiness when we saw the tender care being taken by the sisters attached with this home. We could see vibrancy on the faces of the children and we could also see that all the children were very neat and clean and were very well dressed. These were orphan children and the sisters attached with the home were taking care of these children with utmost care and love. Thus we could experience happiness on our visit to Mother Teresa's Centre of Missionaries of Charity, which was helping financially as well as emotionally for the welfare of young orphan children. We could also see that the dedicated activities being conducted by other staff for taking care of small and big needs of these children. My friend, Vinod, immediately sponsored next days lunch for the children. We both felt very happy and satisfied and I asked the sister attached to the home as to what else they needed. In my next visit, I brought for the home some of the required items for their daily use. I also asked the sister whether do you require blankets etc., for the children and the answer was big No. They were happy, satisfied and contended and we were told that there is adequacy of blankets.

After saying good bye to these young orphan children, we sat in the car, I told Vinod, "Look Vinod, how happy we are after our visit to the Centre set up by Mother Teresa.

Vinod equally was very happy. Although our visit was for a very short period yet in such a short time, our mind became very fresh and all the worries, tensions of the mind, were off from the main stream and we were engrossed at just looking at the activities of this Centre. The best part of the situation is that, at any point of time, whenever I think about our visit to the centre, immediately, I am able to see the vibrant faces of the young orphan children, it gives me happiness. For me, a visit to Mother Teresa Centre brings me happiness. If you would like to experience similar type of happiness also then without any aim, visit one of the charitable institutions run by any charitable organisation in any part of the world and spend some of your quality time there and extend some helping hand and then you will find happiness in your pocket. Well, just give this thought a try and experience the real joy of life.

12. Count Your Blessings and Be Happy

One of the practical formulae of your happiness is to count your blessings showered upon you by the Almighty God. Unfortunately, most of the persons in this world only think about what they have not achieved. What and what they are lacking in their life. Everyone wants to increase his standard of living, increase the quantity of consumer products, but at that point of time, they fail to count the blessings of the Almighty God showered on them. Believe me, when I say that if you spend some time counting the blessings showered upon you by the Almighty God, then definitely, at that point of time, you are going to experience unprecedented happiness. One should endeavour to count the blessings at least three to four times in a year so that your faith is reaffirmed in the blessings which have been showered on you and that you are feeling happy about the same.

When we talk of counting our blessings we should count the blessings showered by the Almighty in different spheres of our life. Hence, when the question comes of counting the blessings offered to you by the Almighty, think of the old time, think of the time when you had no money, think of the time you had no prosperity and compare it with the prosperity which you are enjoying today. This is a blessing which should be counted and then thanks to be offered to the Almighty God. Similarly, think of the blessings showered on you by the Almighty God in the form of children born to you, compare this blessing with the persons many of them who have no children and you are the blessed one with blessings of the Almighty showered on you in the form of children born to you. Likewise, think of the blessings of the Almighty in the sphere of your own educational career, think of the milestones which you have reached and think of the name and fame which you command in your community. It is also time to think about the various activities conducted by you either in social sphere , business sphere or political sphere which have received applause and appreciation from those whom you meet in your day-to-day life. These are the blessings to be counted and then to be happy about.

When I sit down once in a while in a gloomy state and then I count the blessings of the Almighty showered upon me by making me the best youth of India way back in the year 1970 when I was selected by the Lions Clubs International as the best youth of India to attend the World Youth Congress which was held in Atlantic City in USA. Whenever I count this blessing of the Almighty God I feel happy and very happy and my faith in the kingdom of God becomes again strong and strong and vibrant. Similarly, I count the blessings of the God when my first Talk Show was telecast on TV. I also cherish the blessings of the God that I was able to enjoy the wonderful cruise trip to Alaska with me my father and my mother. Definitely, by any standard this is one of the best blessings of the Almighty God showered on me and whenever I think of all these, they inspire me, make me happy and make my life vibrant. Hence, please count your blessings at regular intervals; this is an assured formula for your happiness.

13. Visit a Hospital Lounge on Regular Basis to Reap the Fruits of Happiness

I have found that if you visit the big hospital lounge on a regular basis, you may get happiness. Well, to some readers this idea may appear as trivial idea, as absurd idea or as no idea at all. But the fact remains that you can really derive immense happiness as a result of your constant visit at a big Hospital.

Generally speaking, we visit the hospital only when someone is ill, more specifically only when your own relative or your close business associate or a friend is in hospital. At that point of time only, we visit the hospital. Unfortunately, in this world, everyone now we find is very busy. No one has time at all. The real life fact remains that, even when you visit some one who is admitted in the hospital, you try to reach just 10-15 minutes before the close of the visiting hours so that you stay there for next 10 minutes and you are back home fast. Whether you like to maintain this tight schedule or not that is not the point, but may be due to busy schedule or otherwise we are forced upon to adopt such tactics which save your time.

My suggestion is that one should try to visit a big hospital even when neither relative or a friend is admitted in the said hospital. Try this formula of happiness. I want you to visit the hospital and by your watch just stay 30 minutes in the hospital lobby without any specific aim. You are now visiting the hospital and based on my recommendation, you are sitting in the visitors lobby and you have come at the time when you have no relative admitted in the hospital. Your next question would be what I do now. Well, just let your ears and eyes work. Let your eyes just look around and see what is happening in the four sides of the visitors' gallery and with your ears just listen to the talk which two or more than two persons sitting in the lounge are having. Just half an hour's visit in the hospital lobby will enable you to come to the conclusion that all the persons sitting in this visitors gallery are unhappy because of some health disorder either of the relative or of a family member or a friend. You find all the persons tense, you find all the persons running after the doctor and you find a large number of patients enquiring again and again from the reception help desk about when the doctor will be making the round, you experience the anxiety on the faces of the persons not one or not two but this anxiety is reflected on the faces of all the persons sitting in the hospital lounge of this big hospital. You find in the talk show taking place between some of the relatives of the action plan which should be done at that point of time, especially when their relative is in a critical state of affairs. You will also come across talk going on amongst the visitors about the removal or otherwise of ventilator. You will also come across talk going on between the visitors about discharging the patient and taking him home and just leaving the rest at the mercy of the Almighty God. Well, all this what you are seeing and what you are hearing will enable you to think and to think to be happy. Just imagine that your sitting in the hospital lounge has made your realise that health is the most important and most precious asset of yours. Hence, it is time for you to concentrate on maintaining this costly asset in a perfect manner. The biggest happiness formula therefore is to keep yourself perfectly healthy and next go on to keep your family members very healthy. This is a small little trip but the real life fact remains that if you keep yourself and your family members healthy then you avoid the necessity of visiting the hospital and thus would become instrumental in bringing tons of happiness in your life.

The practical life situation I that when we are healthy one we are able to keep unhappiness a little away from the happiness Chamber of our life.

If you agree on this theme then come forward to start implementation of simple tips to restore the good health of your family members. Firstly, let regular wise and timely eating habits become part of your own life and the extend it to other family members. Don't be effected by emotional disturbances and follow regular health upkeep activities like a regular morning walk, a daily yoga session and finally a balance between work, rest and play. The above formula will keep you healthy and so happy you would be.

14. The Best Gift to Your Parents for Your Happiness

You have one of the best gifts in the world—your parents. Really lucky you are if you have your parents along with you. Just ponder on this theme. The more you think the more happiness you get and you yourself feel that you are really lucky one to be blessed by the Almighty God as you are able to have with you your parents at this time. You may be wondering once in a while to gift some wonderful gift to your parents. Yes, the thought comes to you, especially when you find that you have substantial money power at your command and now at least you can definitely make a wonderful gift to your parents. You enter the big shopping mall and you pick up something very costly and now you would like to present it to your dad or to your mom and you feel happy and you feel satisfied because you have thought of making some good gift to your aged parents. Those who are really very rich may think of gifting away a foreign tour to their retired old parents or they may even give them a spa holiday or someone may like to gift their parents a real luxury cruise holiday of Alaska. Some others might think of making a gift of chauffeur driven car to their parents. The thought of making gift to your parents itself makes you happy. But If you want to have the best happiness for you then it is time to think and ponder about the gift which you can think of making available to your own parents, be it dad or be it mom. I have been thinking on this point for a long time and only the other day my thought came to rest when I read a beautiful thought printed in January edition of Forbes India magazine. It was a thought by Malcolm Forbes. This thought came to him way back in the year 1972. His thought is as under:-

"The wife of one of New York's most eminent lawyers and her sister were discussing what to give their aging, ailing father for Christmas a couple of years ago. 'I'm going to give daddy time — much more time', she said. Her sister later commented to me:' On a moment's reflection, I realized what a wonderful and rare gift that would be.' It's completely true, you know. We love our old folks but have or think we have little time to give them. When one is quite old and has only time, a little bit more of it from friends and loved ones is the most precious gift he can receive and that we can give."

The above mentioned thought of Malcolm Forbes really makes you think and make you think deeper and make you accept the realty of the situation that if you really want your best happiness, then the best gift which you can give to your aging parents is the gift of time. I was myself very much impressed with the thought of Malcolm and I thought I should do introspection of my gift to my aging parents and now frankly, every week I sit down some time and do my own internal audit and come to the conclusion to find out whether the week which has just been completed, was it fine with reference to my happiness formula of giving the gift of my time to my parents. The fact remains that if you and I were to analyse this thought on a regular basis, surely our thinking process would get closer to achieving our objective of deriving more and more happiness by giving time and only time to our aging parent, in particular.

"When I was a boy of 14, my father was so ignorant I could hardly stand to have the old man around. But when I got to 21, I was astonished at how much the old man had learned in seven years." These were the words of Mark Twain and when I read these both quotations viz. Malcolm Forbes and Mark Twain, I find and get a real convincing answer that, yes, the best gift one can give to one's parents is only time. The more time which you give to your parents, the same goes in the process of providing more and more happiness to you, and for your own happiness, especially, from gifting to your aging parent do remember to spend more and more quality time with them which will provide happiness to them and to you together. Also please do remember monetary or materialistic happiness which can be purchased by buying out costly gift is a short term affair and does not last long but quality time which you spend with your parents really lasts long and long and is long time experience for you. It is also an everlasting happiness provider theme for you. Also do remember that while you spend time and while you want to provide that gift to your parents take care of spending more time and spending of time should be with patience. Do not ever lose patience and go on spending quality time with the parents always with patience and patience and only patience. Try to recollect the wonderful journey which your parents had taken with you when you were young and also to take into consideration the patience showered by your parents on you and now it is time for you to repay the same level of patience to your parents.

The other day while I was speaking at a seminar for the benefit of senior citizens the Chief Minister of Delhi, Smt. Sheila Dixit also was of the view that one should try to have meals with the elders in the family specially the senior Citizens. This suggestion given by the Chief Minister reflects the fact that spending of the quality time with the elders would provide them happiness and equally it would boost your happiness fact remains that you can teach this formula of being contended only when you yourself are contended in life. Happiness will be at your command if you are contended.

I remember once the Chairman of Honda Car Company took his grad daughter to the mall as she wanted to buy a pencil. Well, to purchase such a small item it should not have taken long time. But it took them a lot of time. Do you know why ? The grand daughter had selected a very costly pencil but her grand father did not buy her that costly pencil but insisted that she would just take the normal pencil which was cheap and not costly because the purpose and use of both the machines/pencils was the same only. As a young child the grand daughter was not happy and after all she was the grand daughter of the Chairman of Honda Car Co. Now, the Chairman of Honda Car Company explained with logic the purchase of ordinary pencil as the purpose would be served and he also said that this is how he has been running the Honda Car Company for so many decades. This actual life story would inspire you to develop the habit of being contended.

15. Be Contended to Be Happy

Whether you are 18 or 81 and whether you are a man or a woman, one common message for everyone is that if you are contended, you will be happy. Hence try to be contended and develop the art of being contended. It will help in the process of getting near to your happiness for yourself. The theme and concept of contentment would apply at every age of a person. I remember the other day, one of my friend's son was telling his friend that he is very poor because his father sends him to school in an Innova car whereas most of his close friends they drive to school in BMW and Mercedes. Well, this is live example of what we find in the present generation. And then we find that the new generation particularly in today's scenario is not at all contended. If you are not contended in life, surely, the happiness will be a thing of the past and you will not be able to enjoy happiness ever. Therefore, the first message is that you all should be contended and once you are contended then please spread this message of being contended to your children. Believe me, when I say that if you are contended in life, then your life will be easy, simple and you will have no hassles and tensions in facing a tough time which might come up once in your life time, in your life cycle. A contended person is always happy and is away from material possessions. Enjoy life, enjoy the luxuries of life, have money, spend money, but the message is, please be contended with all that you have. Otherwise, a time may come when you will not be able to enjoy luxuries of life, treasures of life which you are possessing today just because you are not contended. Hence, you are going to lose the happiness in this world. These days we find that even the young children, they want to have everything branded, they will like to go in for branded clothes, branded toys and everything costly and branded is their choice. The best fashion brands in the world are on the lips of the children. When you talk of the ladies, the ladies are keeping their eyes to buy a costly bag or costly jewelry. They are not contended with what they are having. Likewise, most of the ladies are not contended with the jewelry which they are having. They want more and much more than what their friends are having. This is a case of not being contended in life. If we are not contended in life, we are unhappy, and please do remember that money cannot buy happiness. It is true money can buy conveniences for your life, but money definitely cannot buy out happiness for you. Please, therefore adopt this 'Mantra' of being contended and then happy person you will be.

I hope that in your own family your children are not contended in life. Like any other parent you would also like to provide the best to your children, but still you experience that the children are not happy. The other day you might have bought a good T-Shirt for your child, but the unhappiness of the child is because you have not bought for him the Ed Hardy branded T-Shirt. You may now tell your son that you will get him his Ed Hardy whenever there is a sale in the Mall. To your this statement the reaction comes instantly from your child who says—"Dad, how miser you are, I need the T-Shirt now and you just to postpone it by next months. These days most of the couples just have one or two children. Now, when you have not bought Ed Hardy T-Shirt for your child, the size of the eyes of your child have become little large, as he has been weeping for a long time and now comes your wife and she tells you to buy out the Ed Hardy T-Shirt for your son. Now, with no choice let you go to the Mall and purchase the costly branded shirt for your child. Once you have purchased the super costly T-Shirt for your child you get to listen some good words from your son. Well, these words are—"Dad you are very cute." So long as you continue to fulfill the wishes of your children you will get to listen to these good words. Just after two months of buying out the costly T Shirt for your son again comes another request from your son for a new Ed Hardy T-Shirt because he was to got to his best friends birthday. Well, what is happening in your family is the out outcome of not being contended in life. It is time now that we teach the mantra of being contended to each and every family member. But the ………..

16. Special Birthday Feast for Your Happiness

Birthday happens to be a very special occasion for each and every person and on your birth day, definitely, you would like to plan a very big party to be thrown open for your friends and relatives. When the birthday date is fast approaching in your calendar, the eyes are stuck on the time of the party, the birthday cake, the preparations, gifts to be received and return gift, if any, to be given. But merely holding a birth day party will not necessarily mean providing happiness to you. The bliss of your life can be seen by you and experienced by you on your birthday, if you hold a special feast on your birthday. Well, you are thinking that what is this feast ? In any case you are surely planning a feast, a wonderful feast, a grand feast, for your dear ones. But I want to show you a slice of that feast on your birthday but with a difference. It will be remembered by you for days together and that feast which will provide you happiness and that feast which will enable you to enjoy the bliss and the big happiness. Well, such type of feast, especially, on your birthday is to invite your blessed ones to lunch or dinner at one of the orphanage, or in hospital or a blind school or a normal school and provide the inmates of these institutions feast, coupled with sweets because today happens to be a great day, a great birthday of yours. Hence, special birthday feast if you organise in the manner mentioned above then surely it will help you in the process of gaining unparalleled happiness for you. This formula of feast on your birthday has been propagated by me for the last many years to various members of my Lions Club. I am happy to place on record that right now hundreds of people throughout India who came in contact with me are taking advantage of deriving great happiness by organising a big feast on their birthday specially in the company of the unprivileged.

In New Delhi, where we live, we organise such birthday feast programme at Chandra Arya Kanya Orphanage home where we have birthday feast with nearly 400 orphan girls. We also invite friends and relatives to join us at this Birthday party with a difference. Likewise, at the famous Blind School located next to Oberoi Hotel in New Delhi we book a lunch or a dinner with the inmates and this type of Birthday Celebration brings in lot of satisfactions and profound happiness. On my parents birthday also we have been having this type of birthday feast programmes. Recently, my sister, Suman, on her 60th birthday, celebrated her birthday in the presence of the inmates of a Senior Citizens Home at Badarpur, New Delhi. The type of happiness which one enjoys can only be experienced but it is very difficult to described it in words. Moreover, this type of special feast leaves an everlasting impression of a great happiness. It is always fresh in your memory lane.

Do encourage your children also to participate in this type of birthday feast programmes for bliss peace and happiness for you and development of the qualities of being compassionate and to share with the less fortunate people of our community.

17. Remove Depression with 'Japa' for Your Health and Happiness

Reciting one single 'mantra' for 10-15 minutes again and again the same mantra, this process is known as 'Japa.' I strongly believe that doing japa should be a part of our daily routine. For all those who are suffering from depression, for them I can say that if you adopt the concept of chanting of the mantra i.e. japa, surely your depression will be a thing of the past. All those persons who are depressed, right now should resort to chanting of mantra. Which mantra to chant? This is your personal choice. You can chant mantra which is dear to you. You can change the mantra or you can keep the same mantra, the effect of the chanting is the same. It has been mentioned very clearly in our scriptures that chanting takes away the negativity in the body and health and once your negativity is out, then it helps you in the process of removing your depression. If you find a person with depression then please suggest him to chant some mantra at least 5 - 20 minutes per day. The more depressed the person is, the more time should he spend out in chanting. You may sit down in a corner room and you can chant alone yourself or if you like you can chant in a group. All those persons who cannot chant alone should go to some temple and with other persons at the time of prayer start chanting the holy mantra in the presence of the Almighty God. Even Doctors have been realising and agreeing to the situation that chanting of the mantra is responsible to overcome depression of a person.

The next question which might crop up in your mind is as to how to do chanting. Well, there are different varieties of chanting. All varieties are fine. However, it is up to you to adopt any particular type of chanting process in which you feel comfortable. Also, please note that while you are chanting, you may close your eyes and continue chanting or you may keep open your eyes and continue chanting. The impact and effect will, however, be same in both the situations. However, my very little experience I can say that chanting by closing your eyes helps you to have a fast reunion with the Almighty God. Hence, better approach is after closing your eyes start your Chanting activity. Still better proposal would be to continue chanting at a fixed time and at a fixed place every day. This process helps in achieving better results of chanting.

Now, let us understand different varieties of Japa or chanting. The first concept is Baikhari Japa. In this concept do chanting with any mantra. You should recite loudly the mantra after closing your eyes. The second type of japa is known as Upanshu Japa. In this type of chanting, you utter the holy mantra but you do not speak loudly. You just whisper and repeat the mantra. This type of japa can also be called as Whisper Japa. The third type of Japa is Mansik Japa or mental chanting. In this concept, any mantra which you want to recite you just recite again and again in your mind. Do not utter any word from your mouth. Hence, do not speak the mantra loudly nor whisper the mantra. Only just repeat the mantra without causing any sound and also without lip movement. The next type of chanting is known as Likhit Japa whereby you can go on writing mantra again and again while reciting the same. Thus, in this Likhit japa concept you speak and chant the mantra simultaneously while you go on writing the mantra again and again. Thus, out of the above varieties of Japa, choose whichever japa or chanting fascinates you. From the point of view of advantage all the concepts are wonderful. It is only one's personal choice as to which japa or which chanting to adopt.

If you want to achieve still better results of chanting, then it is better that couple of your friends or family members sit down and chant for 10-15 minutes. You can even try chanting by your family members alone. In which case the chanting can be done by all the family members sitting together at a fixed time. Some of the persons even complain that while chanting, they are not able to concentrate their mind on the Almighty God. For such persons, the better course is to chant in tune with the CD of the mantra. Hence, if you find that you are not able to concentrate on your chanting, please play the CD or a cassette of the mantra in your house. Play the CD of the mantra in a loud tone and now simultaneously with the loud tone of the mantra on your CD, it is time for you now to repeat the mantra.

18. Forming CCG Group for Your Happiness

We have seen that in real life most of us are not able to prepare a list of just even five friends with whom we can share our worldly real life problems. This happens to be a situation not alone with you, but it is realty with most of the human beings in the whole world. So long you are there ready to offer liberal presents and parties for your friends then you are going to have large number of friends. However, this friendship is hollow friendship and by any standard it cannot be compared to the true friendship. You and I would love to make a large number of friends. Now a days, on the Internet also you are also able to make friends and thereby by being a regular visitor to facebook you find your friends circle ever increasing. In the last couple of years you must have also added couple of new friends, but still the same old fact remains even today, viz., friends and friends everywhere but not a single friend to share your thinking or to share your pain. In this type of a situation, I have been recommending to both men and women to form a CCG group for your own happiness. CCG means Calamity Crisis Group.

Most of the people who are affluent they do not require the monetary help of their friends and relatives but what is most important is emotional help and emotional guidance in hour of crisis. Thus, it is time now for you to screen your friendship circle carefully and take out a small little list of all those persons whom you can rely at the time of your calamity and crisis. I may again mention here that most of the people do not require material help or material support as a friend. Hence, if you prepare your group known as Calamity Crisis Group then slowly this small little CCG group comprising of maximum 3 or 5 persons will be able to extend to you exceptional moral support, moral guidance and moral strength at such point of time when you need the support of a friend in life. The fact remains that money can buy most of the things, but money cannot provide emotional satisfaction, money cannot alone provide bliss, money can surely help in making your life easy and simple, but if you have formed this group surely you will have more peace and happiness at your command. You will be able to have no health related disorder because from outside as well as from inside you are strong. You know that you have the support of the CCG group to help you in hour of crisis. You are aware that members of your own CCG group will come handy to offer guidance and assistance whenever the same is required by you. Forming CCG group is a two way process. While you are looking for support, assistance, advice or a guidance from one or more of your CCG group member, simultaneously you should also be ready to impart your support, help and assistance to the CCG group member as and when the need arises.

The other day, I met a widow. Her husband had expired three months back. The lady had no financial problem at all. Financially she was secured. She had just one problem. The problem was how to keep pace with the daughter-in-law having very rough nature and using abusive language every time she would meet her. All she wanted her CCG group to help her to find a small cottage in Vrindavan or Haridwar where she should would go and stay and lead her balance life in peace. Here comes the importance and utility of CCG that is Calamity Crisis Group. Similar situation may arise in your life in years to come or it may arise for your spouse and at that point of time all that you need is only support, guidance and implementation programme of your desire. Again I may mention here that for all these things no financial support is needed. What is needed is someone to guide and implement your desires at that point of time.

You may not need the support of the members of your CCG group right now and that may be such support may not at all be needed in your life time or may be needed after a decade or two but creating a CCG group right now and continuing to build strong bonds amongst CCG group members would go a long way in bringing hope for you a real fountain of happiness years to come.

I would now invite all my readers irrespective of their age profile to please start forming your own CCG group which will give you happiness in years to come and would provide a good support for you and your spouse in years to come. Do share with me your experience with the CCG group by writing to me at—Subhash Lakhotia, S-228, Greater Kailash Part-2, New Delhi – 110048 (M-09810001665).

19. Group Travel Trip for Your Happiness

One of the wonderful way of making you happy lies in taking long or short trips with friends and relatives instead of participating in the conducted trips. These trips if you undertake, then surely they are going to bring happiness in your life. The moment you are in these trips, you forget all your pains with pleasures in life, emotional set back is a thing of the past and all the hundreds of problem babies are confronted you in your day to day life takes a back seat

Hence, if you want to be happy, take a decision that now onwards you will travel. Generally one feels that if you take a pleasure trip at some destination without any friend or a relative just the two of you, then you feel that you will get a big space and you will be happy. However, I have made a research and I am of the firm view that if you take a group travel plan, then surely your happiness is going to increase manifold. In taking out a group travel plan, your space does not get disturbed because in any case while you are travelling you are not going to stay in a dormitory. Each person is going to get a separate room in the hotel or motel or a resort. Hence, while you are together during the trip, you are also left alone after the end of the day. Hence, please make it a habit to travel in a group. This is one single formula will be instrumental in providing unprecedented happiness for you.

Whether you are alone in life or you are travelling with your spouse and not with grown up children, in all situations it definitely would be a wonderful idea to travel in the group. My thinking that group travel becoming a happiness provider is a reality come true because of many, many trips which I have taken in the last five years in group travel plan. In New Delhi we have one voluntary social organisation by the name of Investors Club. I as the Secretary General of the said Investors Club have tried to propagate the idea of community living through group travelling. Initially, at the start of this concept, the response was not too encouraging but now a days as soon as the group travel programmes are announced by the Investors Club, the same are houseful in less than a week's time from the date of such announcement. This shows the popularity of these programmes and the happiness which the participants derive while going in pleasure trips in groups. Whether you are planning a short trip or you are planning a long trip and similarly whether your trip is planned in India or the trip to some international destination, but the fact remains that in all situations you are definitely going to enjoy and your happiness is bound to increase as a result of group travel trips undertaken by you. I still remember the sweet memories of the group trips undertaken by the members of the Investors Club to Kerala, to Rajasthan, to Sri Lanka, to Egypt, to Finland and many more places. The big fight rather was amongst some members to South Africa who were denied the opportunity to participate in the trip as they were house full because the tours were on first come first served basis.

The big advantage in the group travel plan is that you never become home sick and this becomes one of the important reasons to make you happy while you on a pleasure trip. Moreover, when you are in a group, you do not discuss generally the problem babies which you have left home. Reversely if you are not in a group, then most of the time while you are free, your attention whether consciously or subconsciously devolves around the various family problems and other connected matters of your life. Hence, think now and plan your pleasure trips in such a manner that all your trips in most cases are joint trips which

I guarantee are going to definitely provide you bliss, peace and above all happiness. Your worries and tensions would be a thing of the past if you travel in a group. I remember while we were in Egypt, our group comprised of nearly 60 participants and we all had such a wonderful time that everyone came home very happy. While you are away from home if you are in the group, you feel very much secured and you feel assured of any problem if it arises as the same will be taken care of by other group members. If you also want to be a part of the group travel trip and would like to joint Investors Club, you may please get in touch with me at the following address: The Secretary General, Investors Club, S-228, Greater Kailash Part II, New Delhi – 110048. Mobile: 09810001665.

Even under various other forums whenever we have participated in social group travel plan, we find that happiness had always been at the top of the world. For example the Rajasthani Academy conducted travel programmes to Rajasthan including the programmes at Jaisalmer to witness the world famous desert festivals. The participants at the said desert festival tour appreciated the desert festival. Moreover, cost-wise these tours also become economical because the number of persons participating in the group tours is large. Both combined together the happiness ultimately is at its top. Similarly, under the banner of our Lions Club of New Delhi, Alaknanda, we have been organising at least one pleasure trip a year for the benefit of our members at different locations in India. When I was President of this Lions Club, I organised a similar trip which although was for a short duration of just two days and the visit was just confined to Jaipur, Ajmer and Pushkar. But still ever member came home very happy and every single minute was utilised in the most befitting manner. Hence, do take out time to plan good travel trips for your own happiness and bliss. As far as possible, please avoid taking out group travel trips comprising of business associates or your colleagues in the office. In these types of travel trips the happiness gets restricted mainly because of the fact that as the participants have a common aim connected with business or profession or the colleagues in the office are together in these pleasure trips, hence, of and on some matter concerning business or profession or office activity will be coming up in subconscious mind which will aim at disturbing your inner peace during your pleasure trip. Hence, as far as possible avoid a group trip with office colleagues or business associates.

However, you can always participate in a group travel trip even though connected with business people but particularly if the same is a special trip which comes handy to you on an FF basis which means that the trip comes to you on free fund basis. Yes many times it is seen that your distributor or your principal organises a pleasure trip for the benefit of the key personnel in business or for the business associates, then surely you must participate in these trips because the trip comes to you absolutely free of cost. Next time when you plan your holidays, think on the above theme and try to participate in your travel programme in a group. If you do not have any group now, it is also time now to try to develop either a small or a big group of like minded people with like minded families and like minded eating habits in particular.

This will help you to enjoy your holidays with most happiness. For example, most of the trips which are organise or where I participate the tours are fully vegetarian tours with no hard drinks. This makes it enjoyment at the pleasure trip with like minded persons and presents a family atmosphere full of happiness, enjoyment and care free atmosphere on the other hand. I have noticed that when a couple travels alone they just discuss family matters, family problems but with no solutions. Hence, do try a group holiday for your own happiness.

20. Surgery for Your Happiness

You might never have heard about certain surgeries to be performed for achieving your happiness. But the fact remains that if you adopt the concept of getting into surgery of some portions in the body and mind, then definitely you can aim at achieving better happiness in your life. When we talk about conducting a surgery on some portion of the body or mind, then our emphasis is only with reference to surgery of certain thoughts which prevail in your mind and this surgery of certain thoughts if conducted will result into unprecedented happiness for you which you can experience and which can also be reflected in your behaviour with your friends and relatives.

Many of our readers would be just baffled after reading the above topic. You might have heard about surgery of different parts of your body but might have never come across the concept of surgery for your happiness. Well the fact is that if you resort to surgery of a typical type as mentioned in the following paragraph, then surely you will find happiness in your life. One of the past President of Thrissur Theosophical Lodge once wrote that everybody in this world aspires to a happy life. Most people, however, imagine they must earn more and more money in order to make life happy and secure. This struggle involves unhealthy competition, which is on the increase. Lust for power, jealousy and the craving for material comfort are assuming dangerous proportions, and even violent methods are adopted to achieve these things. Love and friendship are replaced by hypocrisy or what is called diplomacy. Well, when we talk of surgery, I want that surgery should be done of the feelings of jealousy which enter our mind and body. If we are able to perform a surgery to take out jealousy within, then surely you will find more and more happiness in your day to day life. Apart from happiness you will experience a turn around in your health if you adopt the above mentioned formula.

The fact remains that your and my mind is divided into two portions and one portion of the mind is known as the higher mind and another portion is known as lower mind. Your lower mind is dominated by the power of vyasana and that is the reason this lower mind is also known as the desired mind and not one not two but more than two or three desires crop into your lower mind thereby resulting into restlessness in life. Your attitude of developing desires and desires through the help of lower mind brings unhappiness near you. Hence, it is time now to perform a surgery of lower mind to take out desires from this lower mind of yours. Once you take out the desires from your lower mind through the performance of a special surgery, then surely your lower mind will also become empty mind where the absence of desire becomes the way of your life. It is this way of life which you can achieve by performing surgery of your lower mind. This surgery of the lower mind has to be done not with the help of your doctor and also not at all with the help of medical instruments but this surgery which I am talking of your lower mind has to be done by taking up the role of a doctor by yourself and then through surgery removing the desire for seeking in your lower mind. Just imagine if you are able to remove this simple thought of desire, then surely happiness and happiness will be round the corner in all walks of your life and then you will be able to enjoy your existing life style much more. The higher mind is the reversal and the same is not reflected by desire. Take time to develop this higher mind and let your higher mind reach new dimensions in life. Your higher mind is a thinker and it thinks of positive aspects of life. Hence, try to increase the creativity of your higher mind and try to see that your lower mind does not dominate over your thoughts. This simple formula if you adopt my dear friends, then surely you will experience yourself higher levels of happiness. One should always remember that each and every human being is a temple of God and the spirit of God dwells in him. This was also the view of St. Paul. Hence, have faith in the dictum that you are the temple of the living God and the living God you are. This type of thinking if they enter in your mind specially the lower mind, then they supersede the desires coming up in the lower mind of yours and then you feel happiness by making full use of the higher mind of yours. Radha Burnier, International President of the Theosophical Society is of the view that when the basis of freedom is imagined to lie in external conditions, there is a scramble to acquire and enjoy that freedom, for example by means of accumulating wealth. Money only enables a person to do certain things for a time, but it cannot purchase security, happiness, peace or love. Our great spiritual saints whether it was Buddha or Jesus Christ or our Lord Krishna all of them have appreciated the great power of nature and the spirit of compassion guiding the human being. Hence, if you want to be happy, always think of doing at least a little bit surgery of your lower mind and let the higher mind experience bliss of new ideas and new thoughts which will increase your happiness level in a guaranteed manner. Do carry out introspection at regular intervals about the progress of surgery of your lower mind. Just think and it will help.

21. The In-built Formula for Happiness in PC Programmes

You want to be happy, this is a fact and I am also believing your eagerness to be happy which is clearly reflected in your time to read this book. Well when you have taken out your precious time to search for happiness, if you read this book, I guarantee you that yes I will be able to provide you unprecedented happiness with some of the real life practical things and ideas contained in this book. One such idea which constantly gives you happiness relates to taking a decision of having faith in the PC programme for your own happiness. Well when I talk of PC programme, I feel that many of my readers my would immediately get the thinking about some personal computer (PC) lying in office or at your home or some of you may be wandering, then I want to sell you the idea to buy the "Personal Computers" and be attached with the Personal Computers for longer interval. No, not all. My dear friend my magic programmes of happiness is "PC" Happiness Programme. Let me tell you that this programme can be performed by you anywhere in the world. You do not require any trainer to train you in this special PC programme. Also please do remember that my PC Programme comes to you without any training cost or without any purchase of some equipment or instrument or a computer. Well, let me end the suspense. I will straight come to the theme of Subhash Lakhotia's PC programme to provide you guaranteed happiness today and to relish the peace of this happiness in the years to come. My terminology PC stands for not Personal Computer but it stands for "Personalised Charity (PC)." When I talk of Personalised Charity, I mean that let some time of yours be utilised for offering some charity, some help, some assistance to those persons in our society who really need some help or assistance or some guidance. I want you to take up this PC Programme i.e the Personalised Charity Programme on a regular basis and see for yourself how much happiness you are able to multiply. Yes, your happiness will multiply with faster speed which you might not have imagined of. Yes, your happiness will not be for a particular moment. But the bliss of today's happiness can be felt by you even in the future years to come when you sit down and think about today's happiness as a result of PC programme then even in the later years in your life and even in gloomy years of life and even in such time when you are depressed or tensed. If you think and just think about this PC programme undertaken by you, then surely your happiness will rise and rise and experienced by you alone. You do not require any barometer to judge and to find out the quantum of happiness in you as a result of conducting PC programme with your friends. But you can all experience it in a fraction of the second. For those who are new to PC programme and for all those who have never had the occasion to participate in the Personalised Charity Programme may be knowingly or unknowingly the reason may be that such thought has never entered to their upper mind. Then let them now start from day one the PC programme for bliss, peace and above all happiness in every hour of your life.

Now, under the PC programme what I expect you is to extend small little help by way of personalised charity directly to the person who needs it. Please also do remember that this PC programme is not at all a very costly affair. To start with you can start a PC programme just with Rs. 100 and then go on extending it if you receive great happiness in the years to come. The most important point in implementing the PC programme is that the charity which I want you to extend to the poor and the downtrodden should be extended by your own hand only. Hence, I would not feel comfortable if you just write a cheque to some charitable organisation and send the cheque by post. Doing so it is okay. It is good. But it does not bring the advantages of happiness which is to be derived only by extending PC namely Personalised Charity. Now, to start a beginning. Now, to make a beginning. Just buy toffees or chocolates, say just of Rs.100, keep it in a small jar or keep it in the pocket of your coat or a small polythene bag. Now, while making a morning walk or an evening walk and as and when you see small little poor children, take out couple of chocolates from your pocket and give to these children. While you are giving make sure that your hand is focused in giving these toffees in the hands of the participants while your eyes should be focused exclusively in the eyes of the persons receiving the gift of toffees and chocolates from you. When you extend this activity of PC i.e. Personalised Charity, immediately you feel a special rays coming out from the eyes of that child receiving a small little charity from you and coupled with this immediately you find that your eyes turn to the face of that person and your happiness increases very fast because as a result of the personalised charity extended by you, the face becomes vibrant of this young small child who without any expectation has received toffees and chocolates from you. Once you experience the bliss and happiness of extending and participating in the PC formula or a PC programme, then at any point of time in your life when you find that happiness appears to be a thing of the past, then at that point of time please take out some time to extend and continue the PC programme for your own bliss, peace and finally happiness. There are innumerable ways to implement the PC programme. For example just buy a small little balloon or a small not so costly toys and start giving it to the small little poor children which will bring happiness in their day which you can experience and which in turn will definitely provide happiness to you. Similarly, whenever there is a fair or there is a festival in some corner of town or some religious celebration, always take out time to offer some assistance at least to the people who cannot buy anything in this fair by making your happiness investment of say Rs. 50 or Rs.100 or more and then you find that your happiness arrives in your life instantly and this happiness is not lost too far. The happiness continues for a long, long time. I remember a friend of mine who believes in my PC programme, while he went to Mumbai and was having a morning walk on the Marine Drive in Mumbai and he found a stall selling flavoured milk. He tasted the milk. He enjoyed the milk and while he went to place the milk bottle in the dust bin after consuming the same, he found a group of young children ready to extend welcome to the empty bottle which was kept in the dust bin and immediately while the bottle was kept, the children would lift the bottle and take a few drops of milk which remained in the bottle. My friend saw the incident and he was so moved that he ordered for a full bottle of flavoured milk for each and every child. This act of PC programme performed by my friend has provided him unprecedented happiness at that point of time. This is a real story which took place some 10-15 years ago and today my friend is a multi millionaire based in Delhi. When I talk to him while I meet him once in a while, I again ask him to narrate me one happiness formula which he found in his life and immediately he states about this PC programme of offering milk to these poor little young children. Whenever we chat on this issue, immediately I find that my friend starts feeling great pleasure and happiness. This happiness which is reflected in his eyes, in his face, in his smile confirms to me my great faith on The PC programme of happiness. Hence, my dear friend if you really want to be happy, take a solution to spend a small little portion of your income in extending and in carrying out the PC programme namely the Personalised Charity Programme. If you are busy, if you have no time at your disposal, at least take out a solution to confirm to the PC programme at least on your birthday, on your marriage anniversary and then you find happiness in abundant as a result of practical implementation of the PC programme. If you really find some bliss and peace by carrying out the PC programme, please do write to me because your experience will provide happiness to me and will be instrumental in giving your real life happiness story to other friends of mine. Please do remember in this world we should inspire other people, inspire at least for a good cause. I will like to inspire every reader of mine that he or she can get abundance of happiness just by following this PC programme of extending Personalised Charity which can be extended at any point of time in any given situation in any location in the world. Hence, adopt today the Lakhotia PC Programme and let happiness be your friend for a long time. Do write your experience to me at Subhash Lakhotia, S-228, Greater Kailash Part 2, New Delhi – 110048 Mobile 9810001665, E Mail: slakhotia@satyam.net.in . Finally, let me share with you that I am great believer in his concept of PC programme for happiness because I practice it on a regular basis and enjoy the thrill of real happiness on regular basis.

So, why wait. Just buy out an Ice cream or a packet of biscuits or a bag of seasonal fruits for someone and let your mind and body experience the thrill of the real happiness which many of you might not had experienced till date. So, let abundance of happiness be at your door step on a regular basis just with this PC Programme.

22. Meditate on the Theme "Deserve versus Desire" and Be Happy

Sometimes in your day to day life you meet certain persons who are less intelligent than you and on some occasion you also meet persons who are less hard working than you. But when you compare your material prosperity with their material prosperity, you find that their money power is many times higher than your money power. This type of situation results into depression and loss of appetite coupled with loss of happiness. You are unable to find any logic or any reason in the kingdom of God for all that has been happening to you and to the other person. You also fail to understand any reason or logic as to why you should be deprived of higher money power in comparison with persons who are less intelligent than you and also who are not that dutiful to their business activities. Well the first step specially keeping in view your happiness should be that now is the time for you to think and meditate on the concept of deserve versus desire. Your face shows a gloomy picture as and when your desired objectives in life are not fulfilled. Our spiritual heritage specially of India is so great that for ages we have been advocating the concept of the absence of desire for our happiness. Well, the reality is that the absence of desire surely is a way of life and it is the way to the road to happiness, but as we are human being, we find that, it is really difficult for us to completely be away from the concept of the absence of desire. You work, you work hard, you work very hard and then in turn your desire is to make money, a big money and then your desire grows up and you desire to make more and more big, big money. When you make such money, you feel happy and you give all the credit to your acumen and your super intelligence but at times there are situations when you find that in spite of your thinking and in spite of hard working, results have not been forthcoming which makes you unhappy in your day to day life.

However, I have made a great deep research on this theme and I have talked to more than 10000 persons in last ten years and now I come to the conclusion that for your own happiness and for your own bliss so also for your own inner strength it is time now for you to lay greatest faith on the dictum deserve versus desire. This dictum has been coined by me after talking to thousands of people in last couple of years. As I travel and meet new people in new destinations both in India and also outside India, my faith becomes still stronger on this dictum namely the dictum of expecting the concept of deserve versus desire. If you accept this dictum as coming from the words of God, then surely you will have a wonderful time in the in the world of happiness while your depression, anxiety, unhappiness would all be things of the past.

You carry out some activity and you desire the results of that activity keeping in view the efforts both of time and money made by you. For such efforts the results are not in tune with the quantum of efforts, then you fail to understand the reasoning and logic of this type of situation. Well, the fact remains that you may desire a particular activity or a particular result as a result of the efforts put in by you but in the kingdom of God it is only the Almighty God who alone knows the answer in terms of fruits to be awarded to you for the efforts put in by you for a particular activity. Hence, always do have faith in this concept of deserve versus desire. Have faith that in spite of putting the best of time, talent and treasure if certain results are not achieved in life, then it is your desire which is not being fulfilled. But simultaneously do remember that what you have got is all that you deserve in the kingdom of God. Think that what I deserve and what I have got is the answer of the Almighty God and that he alone knows what I should deserve and accordingly he has been kind enough to grant me all that I deserve. Do not let your desire come in between the kingdom of God and let not your desire become supreme and let not your desire prevail over the concept of what you deserve from the hands of God. Hence, whatever you achieve in the worldly life in spite of putting the best effort by you, think that what you have got is all that you really deserve and never ever think of desiring what you want to achieve.

As a human being, I have the right to think of a desire. Yes, you have the right and very rightly you think and express your own emotion and your own desire to yourself. But at the end of the game if you find that your desire remains unfulfilled, then just accept and adopt the dictum of deserve which comes from the Almighty God. If you always adopt this concept and have faith in the dictum deserve versus desire, then surely you will never have any problem of unhappiness in your day to day worldly life.

This concept of deserve versus desire can be implemented in every phase of your life. Whether the matter is in connection with material world or the aspects are relating to family harmony between husband and wife or the mater is connected with relationship between father and son or mother and son or daughter-in-law and mother-in-law, in all situation and in all point of time, always lay emphasis only on this concept of deserve versus desire. Think loudly that yes I have the right to desire something but what I desire if I am unable to achieve that desire, then whatever I have achieved is all that I deserve as per the wishes of the Almighty God. This type of thinking makes you happy and it takes away all negativity in your day-today life. Hence, right from now start and think and think and start on this concept of adopting the wisdom of God through the medium of distinction between deserve versus desire. Do not ever, at any point of time, challenge the action of God.

23. VRS for your Happiness

My next formula for your happiness is VRS. Well, you may think that do I want you to take a Voluntary Retirement Scheme Programme from your job. Oh no, my VRS formula will help you to achieve happiness and that too at such time when you are feeling lonely and you are alone. Whether you are alone or not is not relevant. What is relevant is that at some point of time in life you feel very lonely. You feel scared. You feel that no one is by your side. Well at such moment in life take recourse to VRS Happiness formula. Now, let me tell you that my this concept of VRS means reading the books by Vivekananda, Ram Tirth and Sivanand. Believe me when I say that in hours of gloominess, in hours of depression, in hours when you feel alone, when you feel lonely, when you feel depressed, just sit down, with relaxed mind start reading the spiritual books by Vivekananda, Ram Tirth, Sivanand.

I can tell you my own real life experience way back may be approximately 15 years ago. I was finding some place for peace and happiness. I was feeling lonely. I thought that let me get hold of some spiritual teacher who will inspire me and who will guide me at that point of time. A large number of discourses on spirituality by top spiritual leaders takes place at regular intervals in New Delhi. I attended some of them. But the fact is I could not get what I wanted. Immediately I thought of reading the complete works of Swami Vivekananda which is contained in ten big volumes. I started reading the book one by one and I am happy to inform my readers that I was able to complete the entire reading of all the ten volumes of Swami Vivekananda. As I started reading the book I was able to get inner strength. I was also marking all the important paragraphs and quotations of Swami Vivekananda which were dear to me. At the end of the book I was also writing the important topic on which on a particular page the subject matter was printed in the book. I can only share with you the outcome of this reading and that is that I was able to enjoy great happiness by reading complete works of Vivekananda. The books by Swami Vivekananda are available in English, Hindi and various other languages. However, I opted to read the English version of the book. Later on when I was highly influenced by the writing of Swami Vivekananda I also started donating this set of books by Swami Vivekananda to deserving library and participants. This also provided me great happiness. Now, when I read the complete works of Swami Vivekananda, I was feeling as if I am the new Swami Vivekananda. The great spiritual strength which I derived by reading these spiritual volumes of books by Vivekananda I can only say that if you at any point of time feel that your happiness is at low ebb, then it is time for you to resort to the reading of the books by Swami Vivekananda. Start reading Volume 1 of the Complete works of Swami Vivekananda and stop not and just continue and continue and go on completing Volume 1 then Volume 2 and then conclude by final reading of Volume 10. If you just look at the ten volumes at a time, then may be you will feel disturbed. You may feel worried. You may feel tensed. Then you will not be able to read the whole subject matter. But just go on reading volume by volume para by para and then you find that at most of the time you feel that you are listening to the words of wisdom of Vivekananda right in your own breathing. I strongly believe that reading the books by the top spiritual books would provide Shakti Path to you and would give you strength to be more happy. It is your faith that alone will bring happiness when you start reading the book by Swami Vivekananda. Many times, I receive telephone calls, SMS and E Mail from different corners of the world from people of all age group and who are not known to me expressing their thanks and the benefit derived by them from my spiritual articles and books. When I read, receive these types of messages from my readers, it gives me more strength to share with them all that is coming in my mind to make their life more purposeful, more happy and more blissful. So, my dear friends if you want to be happy and if you want to increase your happiness, then start reading the books by Swami Vivekananda. Apart from providing happiness, the spiritual books by Swami Vivekananda will also give you strength to face this world in a most practical manner. I have in my library complete works of Swami Ram Tirth and as and when I get time I just start reading few pages from his writing. They also inspire a lot specially the small stories written in between the books make very interesting reading. Likewise also read the books by Sivanand. The books by Swami Sivanand are very practical oriented and provide answers to various solutions in life.

VRS is really a blissful formula for your happiness. A special part is that if you read the books by Vivekananda, Ram Tirth or Swami Sivanand, you can read it alone, sitting alone in your office, home, while traveling and at any point of time. These spiritual books by the great spiritual thinkers of India will make your soul little soft and will make your heart more vibrant and more receptive to happiness. Just try and enjoy the benefits.

24. WATS: a Formula for Instant and Guaranteed Happiness

Instant coffee. Oh yes, you may say that you really love it and also you talk about instant reservation and immediately you say yes again because you have been able to get instant reservation either for your pleasure trip or for your business trip while you sit relaxed with your internet connection. But what is more important is to find instant formula for happiness. I strongly believe that WATS is yet another instant formula for guaranteed happiness for you and your family. My formula WATS means "wiping a tear with a smile." If you want your instant happiness and a guaranteed happiness, then one simple formula is also in the form of wiping a tear with a smile. This is a spiritual formula but it has got the great advantage of providing happiness instantly. When we talk of wiping a tear, it does not mean that you take out your handkerchief and start roaming on the roads of your city and someone who is weeping and with your hankerchief, you just wash his tears. This would be the theoretical meaning but what I want is that we should seriously think to wipe the tears of someone who is weeping right now. When you start wiping the tears of someone, make sure that this activity is conducted by you with a smile. You can see and experience the magic of wiping the tears with a smile which will provide happiness instantly for you. Thus, instant as well as guaranteed happiness is assured to all those persons who would like to participate in this programme of wiping a tear with a smile. I recollect actual incident which took place about 18 years ago in Faridabad. I had gone to the office of Faridabad Municipality for some house tax matter. I had parked my car in the parking lot and was on self drive that day as my driver was absent. As soon as I finished the work, I started my car and turned at the gate to pay the parking fee and get back to my home. Horn, and again horn blown by me. Still no way that I could see of the parking boy. Finally I gave a big blow to the horn but still no one to collect the parking fee. However, I could see across the gate the parking man with parking voucher in his hand talking to some fellow. I got down from the car and I scolded the parking boy that why he is wasting my time and why is he not collecting the parking fee. I told him to be little fast. As it was lunch time, hence, I had to go back to my home for lunch with the family. He did not pay attention to my strong abusing language also but I could see that he was talking eye to eye with one gentleman who was in his early forties and with this gentleman was his wife also weeping and there was a young child of about eight years. I saw their faces and somehow I forgot my eagerness to pay the parking fee and to rush home. Reversely I now asked the parking boy as to what the situation was and why this couple were weeping. The parking boy told me that this couple had come from some far away village to Faridabad town but they had lost their purse containing money and now they had no money to go back to their village. Before I could answer anything the parking boy was grumbling to himself and was repeating the words that okay in next half an hour it will be lunch break and then he continued speaking I will talk to every peon, every servant, every clerk in the office and collect from each one two rupees, five rupees or ten rupees and then give money to this poor villager who has lost his purse so that he can go home. I listened this statement of the parking boy and again posed my eyes directly into the eyes of this couple. In my inner heart the conclusion came that yes genuinely they have lost their money purse and they are in trouble. I was also feeling very happy with the type of thinking of the parking boy and his thought and his thoughtful vision of helping this couple by arranging funds from all persons at the lunch break. Immediately I took out from my purse Rs. 200 and gave away to the weeping couple and told them that you eat something now. It is lunch time. Take some biscuits for your son and then you proceed to your village by the bus. Immediately I could see the falling tears from the eyes of the couple instantly and they were just steering at me. I was feeling very happy. This is one small little example of deriving happiness by "wiping the tears with a smile." If you want to enjoy the bliss of instant and guaranteed happiness, then please play the role of wiping the tears of someone but always do remember that when you are wiping the tears of someone it should always be done with a smile only.

When we talk of wiping the tears for our own happiness, I would like to just add for the benefit of my readers that this does not cost a big monetary expense. It is only your thought and financial assistance coupled with guidance that can make wonders in wiping the tears of someone who is in distress, who is in problem and in turn you receive your instant happiness in a guaranteed manner.

Many times wiping a tear can also be done without any financial expenditure. May be someone is in need of some answer, some solution, some medical advice, some route to follow or any other such matter which may not involve parting with your money but just some answers from you with a smile can bring tears for someone and which in turn can bring the starting of instant happiness for you. Follow this and enjoy the experience of a small little financial assistance from your end to wipe the tears of some to increase your happiness instantly and in a guaranteed manner.

25. Faith in God Can Relieve Your Body Pain and Get Back Your Lost Happiness

Medical science has advanced in the country. New research is being conducted day in and day out not merely in India but in the whole world. The object of the new research is to provide new vistas of relieving pain to you. However, I strongly believe that if you have great faith in God, then you can get relief of your body pain without any hassles and tensions at all.

Spiritual healing is one of the process by which you lay faith on the Almighty God and your thinking about the theme that yes God has come to help me, God has come to relieve my pain, God is surely going to cure me, God cannot give more trouble to me, God cannot give continuous pain to me, this thinking will bring miracles in your own life time and you will be able to experience the miracles of faith in the Almighty God. Believe me when I say that the pain, the displeasure, the problems in life can all be solved by having faith in the kingdom of God. When we talk of faith I would like to have unflinching faith without any ifs and buts. Hence, do have faith in the Almighty God to relieve your pain and misery in your life.

I remember nearly 20 years ago my own younger brother who himself is a doctor was passing through some medical problem and at that time my father gave him a wonderful quotation by Amil Kue which read as follows: Day by day in every way I am getting better and better. By reading this quotation everyday inner strength was derived by him. My father continues to give a printed copy of this quotation to all those who have problems. Even the above quotation framed in a wonderful placard was presented by my father to many persons who well ill on the occasion of centenary celebration of my late grandfather Shri Mohan Lalji Lakhotia in the year 1999-2000. If you have faith in the above dictum, you will surely be able to come out from your body pain from your other illnesses specially if the above quotation is read with a further addendum to say that with God's grace definitely day by day in every way I am getting better and better. Then surely you will find that your prayers have been answered by the Almighty God. Your pain of the body or any other problem baby relating to health will diminish day in and day out. I remember to have read a research report by the Oxford University scientists with reference to faith in God. The said research report said that if you have faith in God, you can relieve pain. The research conducted by this group on the patients said that even painting of GOD by the patient was responsible for pain relief to them. I would like to give my readers a real practical suggestion for enjoying happiness and that is, please place a photograph of God near your bed and let a thought come in your mind which should be expressed by you through your words that—God is near me, then how can pain come near to me. This type of thinking will make you pain vanish and will make you happy.

26. Positive Thinking: a Yes Formula for Your happiness

Always be positive and let negativity never enter your mind zone. Do remember that this is a sure success formula for your own happiness. There may be innumerable instances in your life whereby certain action or inaction not by you but by persons associated with your working or persons coming under your control might bring mental problems for you. These types of activities by persons associated with you may induce negative thinking at your end. But if you want your own bliss and your own happiness, then always have a positive thinking attitude and this will be your number one formula for definite peace for you. I remember a Chinese phrase: Happiness is someone to love, something to work at and something to hope for. Now, if we analyse this Chinese formula in our day to day life, we definitely come to the conclusion that we should carry on our activity with love, with happiness and we should always be positive while we are at work. The work may be business or professional work or the work may be family activity or relaxation work. However, in every activity which you are engaged in, always have a positive thinking attitude which will bring a guaranteed happiness in you life. Love and work is the simple dictum for maintaining a positive thinking in your life. Love your work and carry on your work with positive thinking. Then you find that there is no going back from the pond of happiness in your life.

One of the trustees of Vikram Sarabhai Foundation once gave an example of a woman in a Bangalore slum who had migrated from a village in the interior of Karnataka. She works fourteen hours a day on a construction site, lives with six other people in an ill smelling, single room hut and eats, if at all, stale food in a tin plate. Yet she rejects the idea of life being better in her village with surprised astonishment. Why? Not because of better material conditions, although she might answer it that way. For the first time, she can feel the future in her hands, has hope of a better life for her children. Hope is the almost somatic conviction that there is a hidden, even if unknown, order to our visible world. That there is a design to life which can be trusted in spite of life's sorrows, cruelties and injustices. The cynic might see the presence of hope in the poverty-stricken women in the slum as completely unrealistic, look at her as someone who clutches at the thinnest of straws , who has never learnt that there is something as hoping too much, or hoping in vain. But what keeps this woman, and so many millions of others cheerful and expectant even under the most adverse economic, social and political circumstances is precisely this hope which is a sense of possession of the future, however distant that future may be.

A question sometimes arises as to how can one have a positive thinking and a positive attitude specially at the time of being surrounded by day to day life problems. Well, it is the attitude and thinking which can bring positive attitude in you at all times of your life. In the first stage the simple formula is that you should have a faith in the concept of positive thinking which brings you nearer to the real happiness in life. Once you have this type of attitude, only then it will be possible for you to be positive in all situation at all times and in all crisis situations.

Sometimes we start comparing ourselves with others and then may be we may come across a situation whereby we find that we are better off in all circumstances in comparison with some other person. But still we do not get that much respect or regard or affection from our community. Well, this type of activity might result into a negative thinking and this negative thinking will take away your creativity and will push us into the back door of anxiety and depression whereas the correct answer is to have a positive thinking and try to develop once again your power, your personality, your attitude, your knowledge and aim for the best. Do not be happy just by comparing with others.

27. Kaya Kalpa for Your Health

Various innovative ideas, therapy, messages you are looking at to make your good health. Well, one single objective at looking at different therapies is to find something new which can bring better health for you. It is a well known fact that in the recent past much thrust has been there in the use of Aromatherapy and the Herbal Massage. It is a fact that Aromatherapy and the Herbal Massage etc. are all contained in our ancient wisdom and therefore they are recognised as modern healing tools. The essential oil helps in the process of better health of a person. One can see the pictures of medicinal plants on the caves of Lascaus in France and these pictures are from Eighteen Thousand BC. Thus, it is very clear that essential oils right from old age has been instrumental in bringing better health specially in old age. If you are interested to have fresh odor from your body, then remember that is the sign of a healthy person in you. When I went to Egypt two years back I was happy to find that even 4000 BC we can find the stories of perfumed oil etc. which go in the process of helping better health of a person. In India the Ayurveda concept recognises the importance of massage with the essential oils and innumerable health advantages are associated with the use of different types of essential oils. Now a days even essential oil packages are being made available in the market. One single advantage of use of Aromatherapy with the aid of essential oil is to have better health enhancement at all times. The mind, the body and the soul also get enriched as a result of various Ayurvedic treatments coupled with use of herbal oil, herbal paste etc. One should consult an expert on the subject of Ayurveda and thereafter start implementing and practising the precept and practise relating to health related usage of essential oils

Aromatherapy. Long ago may be hundreds of years ago the life was simple and people lived in the kingdom of happiness and health but with the advancement of new technologies new problems started creeping in the life of the humanity and then started the problems connected with health and happiness. Flourishing we are in industry, flourishing we are in art, flourishing we are in new technological advancement but while we are materially flourishing, the fact remains that our health and happiness kingdom is diminishing the quality of our happiness coupled with the quality of our health is taking a back gear in these years. But I feel that the use of Ayurveda therapy which fortunately has no side affect or disadvantage can be applied with success for reaping the fruits for your health. I remember the actual life story of Tapaswiji Maharaj which has been quoted by Dr. Light Miller and Dr. Bryan Miller in their book entitled Ayurveda and Aromatherapy. They mentioned about a real life incident of Tapaswiji Maharaj. It is mentioned in the book that born a prince in a Sikh kingdom in northern India, Tapaswiji Maharaj was trained to be a military leader, and assumed the role upon his father passing. At the age of 55, he tragically lost all his immediate family, and in his devastation renounced all worldly possessions.

He found a guru, learned many yoga practices, and began to live a severe, austere life. He lived in a cave without food for six years, subjecting his body to extremes of heat and cold, and holding uncomfortable postures for long periods of time. During one twenty-four-year period, he remained standing or working with his left hand over his head. He spent periods of three, seven, and eight years standing in a single spot. For twelve years he spent six hours a night meditating by a freeing lake wearing only a loin cloth while his disciples poured buckets of frigid water over his head. Those twelve summers he spent six hours each day in the scorching sun, surrounded by a ring of fire.

By the time he reached 100, his body was ruined; partially deaf and blind, no teeth, bent over at the waist, using a cane to walk, he prepared to die. On his final journey, he met a Yogi who, sensing his spiritual greatness, convinced him to undergo 90 days of kaya kalpa. He emerged looking like a man of thirty, with black hair, new teeth, and a supple strong body. After returning the favor to the Yogi (90 days of kaya kalpa service), he set out on even more austere practices. Twice more during his long life, he underwent kaya kalpa to rejuvenate his battered body, allowing him to travel, teach and demonstrate spiritual attainment and detachment to thousands.

At age 185, he demonstrated his final control over his weak, diseased and wasted body; he momentarily transformed himself into an erect, strong and radiant being, chanted the sacred AUM, and died instantly.

I must have read the above mentioned real life story about the incredible life of Tapaswiji Maharaj at least one dozen occasions. Every time when I read the above story, I get inspired and I feel like taking out some research whereby we can go into the detailed aspects of kaya kalpa for achieving a robust health of our own. The said Tapaswiji Maharaj was born in the year 1770 and he expired in the year 1955. I am also planning to visit the exact destination or village where Tapaswiji Maharaj lived in north India. If I can get a view of that, I would definitely be happy to go and try to explore some more facts to find by research the details of the kaya kalpa undertaken by Tapaswiji Maharaj which resulted into his complete transformation and a robust healthy body.

However, I strongly believe that taking advantage of the body transformation activity through the concept of kaya kalpa it is possible for us to regain our lost health and live a long life. I am inspired by the above mentioned book written by Dr. Miller and the book inspires me and arouses my faith in the concept of kaya kalpa. Dr. Miller also writes in the said book that ten thousand years ago, a king of India had a problematic, headstrong daughter, who refused to marry any of the eligible princes who were presented to her. In anger and frustration, the king decreed that she was to be blindfolded and placed in the castle courtyard in the midst of all her suitors. The man she touched was to be her husband and their children would continue the royal line.

On that day an elderly holy man wandered into the courtyard to deliver herb to the king's physician and, by chance, was touched first by the princess. Even though he pled exemption due to his advanced age and holy vows, the King's word was law and they were to marry in three months time. The holy man consulted his teacher about his problem, and the teacher instituted an intensive programme to rejuvenate and energise.

For 90 days the holy man ate a special diet, performed breathing techniques, took ritual herbal baths and was anointed with sacred oils. At the end of that time his hair had turned from gray to black, a new set of teeth had grown into his mouth, and his skin and body were youthful and strong. He married the Princess. They had many children and lived happily ever after. This was the beginning of kaya kalpa (bodies' transformation), a secret healing technique used in India for thousands of years by religious healers to rejuvenate and give longevity to royalty and holy sages. Vigorously suppressed by the British, this knowledge was almost lost. There are now only 18 practitioners left in the world; fortunately, in a form more appropriate to Western life styles. In addition to its rejuvenating qualities, kaya kalpa is useful in expanding awareness, consciousness, and can be an aid in making decisions and life changes.

If you have faith in the writing of Dr. Miller, then make an extensive reading of his book Ayurveda and Aromatherapy and thereafter start practicing and preaching the concept of kaya kalpa which is possible to bring better health for everyone. Dr. Miller's book presents a great research on Aromatherapy and Ayurveda. I also get great faith in the writings of Dr. Miller.

Do explore the various Ayurveda therapies, provide kaya kalpa for you and for your health transformation. The first thing is to have faith in this concept and then to do research and read and read more about Ayurveda, about essential oils and then under the guidance of a recognised Ayurveda expert following and practising these Ayurveda recipes for your own kaya kalpa.

28. Avoid A3 for Your Own Health and Happiness

If I say that you want happiness to enter in your life domain. This fact is a certainty and that is the reason why you are going through this book by taking out some of your valuable time. Now is the time to avoid A3 activity for your robust health. These A3 activities are anger, then anxiety, then apprehension. Hence, if you want to be healthy and happy, please delete from your mind dictionary all about the anger activities with which you are connected and also let lose the anxiety in your body and finally do not care much for apprehension in your life. If you just take care of these "A3" programmes and make it a habit of not let in come of the three A3 items in your mind and body, then surely you are going to witness a healthy body for you and no doubt it is a fact that if the body is healthy, you derive more and more happiness.

Never ever become angry. If you are angry, your creativity gets lost. Your thinking ability vanishes and when you are angry, you feel unhappiness all the time. You will never come across a person in your whole life time who is angry and still happy at that time. Try to observe a person who is angry and at that point of time see if he is happy. The answer always will be in the negative. The fact remains that is a person cannot be happy and a person cannot be healthy if he is angry. Hence, avoid anger at every cost in your life. If a person is angry, he just burns himself, not necessarily outworldly but definitely inworldly. You are burning yourself when you are angry. You should always think and meditate and pray to the Almighty God to grant you strength so that you are away at least 100 kms. away from the dragon of anger. If you are able to control anger, you will become popular. If you are popular, your happiness will increase. Hence, don't let anger come near you at any stage in life. It is true that some action and some activity by others makes you angry, it is true but the fact is that you alone will have to conquer your own anger if you want bliss, peace and happiness and a better healthy life. Hence, avoid anger at any cost in your life.

Anxiety takes away your health and happiness. You must have seen that many persons who are having anxiety in their body, they are not able to have good sleep. Such persons are also not able to have a good digestive system. Hence, surrender to God and let anxiety be out from your body zone. It might appear to say this statement in a simple language but you may say that it is very difficult to follow it. Yes, difficult it is. But if you just practice and if you just think that your anxiety is going to take away your health, then you will understand the importance and thereafter you will avoid all the activities concerned with manufacturing anxiety in you. Have faith in God. Do your work. Be devoted and dedicated to your work related activities. Have faith in the thinking and working of the God and then you find that anxiety is a thing of the past. Try to see that your anxiety zone is removed from your body. If you are having anxiety, you will find tension will be the next sister to come close to anxiety and running away will be your food taste and mental peace. Therefore, avoid always anxiety. I have found out from my own life experience that in last nearly 40 years that once can overcome anxiety if one adopts to systematic working and scheduling and programming one's own activities of life. I feel it is time for you now to plan your activities to avoid anxiety at every cost. My lesson in anxiety free life has been taught to me by my father Shri Ram Niwasji Lakhotia.

Away from apprehension should be your focused mind dictum. What will happen tomorrow, what will happen if a particular activity does not take place, when I am on tour whether I will get the order or not, what if my employer were to sack me, will I get the job, am I expected to get increment next year, whether I will be able to continue to make payment of my EMI for house property, whether the car will be taken away and lifted by the bank for nonpayment of my car installment, my child is going to school what happens if he falls ill in the school or if he meets with an accident while crossing the school or is hurt by a friend in the bus. These are just to name a few of the items which may crop up in your mind which if you think will block your mind because of your apprehension. Well, thinking about apprehension and thinking about what has not yet happened is no good for your health. Stop thinking of all action and all activities which have not taken place. I know, the other day some of our friends were to catch up early morning flight for going to Kerala for a pleasure trip. The flight was in the early morning and my friends were in the habit of getting up late in the morning. I remember right from 9 P.M. onwards they would force me again and again to request me that I should wake up them in the morning. They have also made a reminder on the telephone for alarm bell. They also logged in into the time alarm in the mobile phone and they told the servant also to wake them up in the early morning as they were to take the morning flight. However, they were continuously having apprehension that they might miss the morning flight and what happens if they miss the morning flight was their problem coming to them again and again. I advised my friends that they should completely relax and take a good sleep because they have already taken action plan to wake them up. But because it continued with unexpected apprehension, hence they were not able to sleep well in the night and they would wake up every hour or two and see the clock and again try to take a sleep. If you are also in the habit of getting involved with apprehension in life, then please remember that it is time now to change for better and change so as to get better happiness and better health. Just remember that from now onwards do not ever have apprehension for all that has not yet happened in your life. Adopt work action plan. Be relaxed. Carry on your activities and just say good bye to anger, anxiety and apprehension and see how health and happiness are at your command.

29. It Must Be Ready for Your Ego

If you are a person with ego·fading your body, then surely happiness cannot enter your life. It is an acknowledged fact that in your day to day life either you may keep ego at your side or you may keep happiness. Hence, the best way to achieve happiness is to keep ego away from you. Unfortunately most of the persons who are egoistic persons never accept the fact that they are egoistic. You may be egoistic, no problem, but first of all accept the reality of the situation, accept that yes you are egoistic and then try to remove and wash away your egoism in due course. You benefit only if you accept in reality the possession of ego. Then only the second question comes of removing your ego with brush. The happy atmosphere whether in a family or in a social organisation or business organisation can come to a halt just because of your ego.

I remember long back some thirty years ago it was ego which was responsible for complete closing down of one of the units of an international service club organisation. Hence, always keep in mind that if you want happiness, then you will have to throw your ego in the dust bin. Make full use of your dust bin and use dust bin to throw away the ego in you.

An egoistic person cannot achieve the benefits of happiness in life. Hence, think now, act from today and just keep your ego in your dust bin and get ready to experience this happiness. The following **WISE VERSES *ARE* FOR YOUR HAPPINESS** which I received from a friend of mine and which I want you to benefit from. Here they are :

- *God wants spiritual fruit, not religious nuts.*
- *Dear God: I have a problem. Sometimes, It's me.*
- *Growing old is inevitable, growing up is optional.*
- *There is no key to happiness. The door is always open.*
- *Silence is often misinterpreted, but never misquoted.*
- *Do Mathematics. Count your blessings.*
- *Faith is the ability not to panic.*
- *Laugh every day, It's like Inner jogging.*
- *If we worry, we probably don't pray. If we pray, we probably won't worry.*
- *As a child of God, prayer is kind of calling home every day.*
- *Blessed are the flexible, for they shall not be bent out shape.*
- *The most important things at our homes are the people.*
- *When we get tangled up in our problems, be still. God wants us to be still so He can untangle the knots for us.*
- *A grudge is a heavy thing to carry.*
- *He who dies with the most toys is still dead and who knows where he has gone?*
- *We do not remember days, but moments. Life moves too fast, so enjoy the precious moments.*
- *Nothing is real to you until you experience it, otherwise it's just a hearsay.*
- *Surviving and living our life successfully requires courage.*

30. Cancel Your Appointment with Mr. PHJ

If you want to experience the happiness in your life, then definitely you will have to cancel all your appointments with Mr. PHJ. Well, you are ready to cancel the appointments specially if it brings happiness in your life. But the point is you must be wondering as to who is this Mr. PHJ. Well, it is this Mr. PHJ with whom if you cancel appointments, then surely your lost happiness will enter your life and here comes Mr. PHJ's full name—it is Prejudices, it is Hatred and it is Jealousy.

Hence, if you pay attention today to do away with prejudices and hatred against someone and finally if you delete jealousy from your day to day life, then you will find that your health and happiness is at its best. Hence, it is time now for you to plan and plan your own life in such a manner that you are never prejudiced against any person whom you meet in different walks of life.

Similarly, you may not be happy with the action of someone. You may not be happy with the working style of someone. But that does not mean that you should have hatred for that person. If you posses hatred for someone, then it is this hatred which is responsible for removal of happiness from your life.

Finally, reason or no reason one should completely avoid jealousy towards other human beings. Sometimes you may yourself justify your action of being jealous. But the fact remains that at any point of time under no circumstances jealousy can be accepted and appreciated.

Thus, if you decide not to have jealousy within you, then surely your life will see all round robust health for you and better happiness in your day to day activities.

The following lines of Edward Payson Powell may perhaps inspire you:

The Old Year has gone
Let the dead past bury
Its own dead. The New
Year has taken possession
Of the clock of time
All hail the duties and
Possibilities of the coming
Twelve months!

31. Keep Formula FF in Your Crown

Only if you want to achieve better health and happiness for you in whole of your life, then it is time now for you to keep this formula FF in your crown of life. Formula FF means "forget and forgive." It is a well known fact that in our daily life we come across various incidents in life. Someone might have committed a mistake. Someone might have committed as blunder and someone according to you might have committed the greatest mistake in life. But at that point of time if you adopt the theme of forgetting and forgiving a person, then the biggest advantage of adopting this concept is available only to you and you alone because once you adopt this concept of forget and forgive, your mind becomes calm and clean.

Your inner faculty starts shining and you are not baffled by the wrongs being done by someone in your life because you have committed yourself to adopt the concept of forget and forgive. Hence, if you keep handy this concept of forget and forgive in your crown, then you have no stress at any point of time and happiness will be in your life all the time.

Even in business we find that all those businessman, traders and professional persons who do not accept the concept of forget and forgive, they are always under stress. They always remember the wrong done by someone in business. They always remember the unfair trade business activities undertaken by someone and that they are never ready to forgive anyone.

Do remember that when you are not ready to forget and forgive in life may be in business, then at any point of time even when you are concentrating on your business activity, you find that your mind is disturbed, perturbed and this is surely going to affect your health. Your health is no good. Happiness then is definitely bound to be a kilometer away.

Hence, in your life time do remember to keep in your crown this concept of forget and forgive and experience for yourself the bliss, peace and happiness in your own life which you can experience every moment in your life.

32. Meditate on Your Life Mission and Be Happy

Sit down in a cool place and this cool place can be in any corner of your house or the public park in your colony or it could even be a secluded place away from your home. Now, in this calm and quite atmosphere think and meditate at least for sometime about your own life mission. Apparently at first go this theme may not appeal you. Similarly, at one point of time you may think that oh I am very intelligent. I know my mission. I am fast go thinker. I am grown up. I am already acting in tune with the mission of my life. Well what you think may be true but if you really want to experience happiness in your life, then it is time for you to mediate at least for an hour or two and in this meditation even you can carry out the meditation with eyes open and a pen and paper or a diary in your hand. Now, think with concentrated mind about the mission and aim of your life. Just not think mentally. What you think, transcribe it on a piece of paper, pose for ten minutes and again start rethinking and again read what you have written about the mission of your life and then finally edit what you have written and then comes the still clear picture of the mission of your own life. Once you prepare this type of statement (mission statement), then surely you will find that your happiness quantity would increase and then you will be able to keep yourself happy for a much longer time and this is mainly possible because of the fact that you have devoted time to think about your mission in life and now you are acting in tune with your own thinking about your own mission. Hence, make it a habit at least once in a year to meditate on your life mission and then start experiencing higher dose of happiness in your life time.

33. The Blissful Silence for the Blissful Happiness

Think of silence, complete silence at least for couple of hours in a day. This is the formula to bring your happiness specially if you are a person who is not happy at least for some portion of time in a day. But if you are a person who is normally not happy, then to get your happiness and really to get your lost happiness, it is time for you to adopt the concept of blissful silence at least for 24 hours and that too once in a month. The day when you are observing the blissful silence for 24 hours then I want you to completely keep quite. You can continue with all your normal activities of life but just don't use your mouth on that day. Briefly what I want is that you should not speak even a single word for 24 hours. This sounds very difficult. Yes it sounds difficult. But when you are ready to take this difficult proposition in your life, namely to be completely silent for 24 hours at least in a month, then surely you will experience the unprecedented bliss and happiness in your own life. What I say is not a theory and what I say is experienced by thousands and the experience which I have myself accepted, found, understood and realised in my own life. I want all my readers to take advantage of this experience of life and start practising 24 hours silence which is known as "Maun" in our spiritual language. You may carry out this activity of remaining 24 hours in silence at your residence while you are on a holiday or at any other place and on any day your choice. There is no fixed timing to start your 24 hour silence programme nor there is any fixed particular day on which you should start this activity. But the fact of life is that if you adopt this concept of 24 hours complete silence, then surely it is going to bring better happiness formulas in your life. Hence, resolve today to start one day silence at least in a month. Let me tell you that it was Mahatma Gandhi, the father of the nation who used to adopt this same concept of blissful silence for 24 hours on every Monday of the week. Yes, every Monday Mahatma Gandhi would not talk to anyone for 24 hours. He would still carry out his activities but not talk to anyone. If you want happiness to enter your life zone, then it is time for you now to adopt this concept of staying completely in silence for 24 hours and then see with your own experience the quantity of happiness which has increased in your life. I also read that when Mahatma Gandhi used to adopt the concept of complete silence for 24 hours and on that day supposing some foreign dignitaries were to visit his Ashram in Ahmedabad, they would still not talk to him. They would just write and then discuss the matter. I am very much confident that this quality of Mahatma Gandhi namely to keep complete silence made him really achieve great heights in happiness.

If you find difficult in adopting this formula of adopting complete silence for 24 hours at a stretch, then at least try to be in complete silence for 6 hours time and then increase this gradually to 24 hours. See the benefit. If by adopting 24 hours complete silence you drive more happiness then please do not forget to write to me your own experience of achieving happiness as a result of increasing your blissful silence in day to day life.

If you experience the bliss, the peace, the happiness, then please extend this formula to your family members, relatives, friends and business associates.

I remember couple of years ago as Secretary General of the Investors Club for the first time I had organised a special camp known as 24 Hours Silence Camp and then I took a group of more than 100 persons to the Brahmakumaris Ashram near Gurgaon and let me place on record that 100%

participants had adopted with success this concept of blissful silence for 24 hours and what their reactions were, they were just amazing. Almost every participant was experiencing more happiness, more bliss and better health.

If you want to adopt it, it is time for you now to adopt this concept which requires no expense and no special preparations.

34. Don't Play with the Emotions of Others

Control your emotions and let not emotions control you, this is the dictum given by me to a large number of my spiritual friends and that I have found in my life that if you are emotionally happy, then you are happy in your life also. I would like to strongly recommend to all my readers that they should never ever play with the emotions of someone else.

If you play with the emotions of some other person, if you hurt him, then the rays and the waves coming out from that person which you may not be able to easily see but they will take away your happiness.

Do believe in this concept and once you believe in this concept, then surely you will find that yes your happiness increases if you do not play with the emotions of someone else.

Many times it may appear to you that you are not playing with anyone's emotions. But still someone else may think that you are otherwise playing with his emotion. In that situation just think and concentrate on the situation existing with reference to the circumstances and situations prevailing between you and the other person and see whether knowingly or unknowingly you have been instrumental in playing with the emotions of that other person, if the answer is positive, then just rectify your mistake and stop this habit of playing with the emotions of someone.

Always have the idea in your mind not to hurt someone. This hurt may not be a physical hurt but may be the hurt with your tongue.

Hence, always when you speak, be careful and keep

your tongue under control.

Let your tongue not disturb the emotions of your acquaintances. Otherwise it will definitely be instrumental in reducing happiness.

So, if you want to be happy, always do remember that you should never play with the emotions of someone else.

35. Stop Show-off for Your Happiness

While you go on reading the pages of this book, one thing which is crystal clear is that you are interested in getting more of your happiness in your life time and that is the reason it shows your seriousness to read something more about health and happiness. One of the important formulas and the practical formula for increasing your happiness is to stop showing off. Knowingly or unknowingly if you adopt the habit of show off amongst your known people, then it can be a major cause of unhappiness in your life. Generally, it is seen that persons show off their wealth in the presence of their poor relatives or their friends or amongst their business acquaintances. Your habit of show off may result into constant unhappiness in your life.

This unhappiness may enter specially when you find that consequent to your concept of show off you find that your other friends, relatives or acquaintances are also adopting this same concept of show off. When your friends and acquaintances also adopt the concept of show off, then you find a perplex situation near your eyes because you find that others are show offing their possessions in life, be it jewellry, car, house, farm house etc., etc. Now, to cope up with the increased show off by others you are finding yourself constantly under great tension. The best solution is therefore never to show off. If you adopt this formula of never to show off, then the great big advantage can be experienced by yourself in your own life. Never have comparisons specially for materialistic world. If you want to have comparison, have comparison with reference to how soft spoken you are, how kind hearted person you are, how charitable disposed you are. But just don't compare for the day to day luxuries of life. Your comparison with others makes you unhappy, realise it, adopt it and stop it and then you see for your own the big advantage of better happiness in your life.

Even when you are young, you find that getting comparisons with reference to the dress, the mobile phone, the shoes and the hair style might have been responsible for bringing at one point of time some happiness in you because you find in yourself a superior person with reference to these items in comparison with your school mate, college mate or a friend. Suddenly, some day one of your friend is seen better well dressed than you are, has a big costly watch and has a new mobile phone, in that situation when you see this happening near your eyes, you get depressed. Your health gets down. Your happiness vanishes.

Hence, the best formula is never to show off to your friends, relatives or to anyone else. We find this concept of show off becoming strain for your health specially in the case of ladies going to a kitty party. To put a better impression amongst your friends in the kitty party you are very meticulously dressed and you try to see that each time at a kitty party you wear a new dress and not just dress but some new jewellry. The day you find that you have not been able to do this, then that day onwards starts your unhappiness.

My advice therefore to all those going to the kitty party is never to show off amongst your kitty party friends either with reference to dress or jewellry or anything else. I remember one of my friend's wife. She was a member of a Kitty for last three years and at every kitty meet you will find her dressed in a new dress and with new jewellry. The other day my friend complained to me that as his wife is interested to have show off a new piece of jewellry at every meeting of kitty party. For this purpose what she was doing was to sell her jewellry and exchange it with some other jewellry from the jeweller and this she was doing it on continuous basis. But unfortunately by doing this activity of exchanging jewellry with the jeweler for being used at every new kitty party she did not realise that the overall gross weight of the jewellry got reduced because at every time whenever the new jewellry was repurchased, the jeweller would deduct a substantial percentage out of the gross weight and finally after three years my friend's wife found that out of the total stock of her jewellry at least half the jewellry has vanished and this vanishing activity took place just because of changing and making and remaking and changing of the jewelry for every kitty party.

 If you want to make money, if you want jewellry to be safe, if you want your happiness to grow, then it is time now to do away with this activity of show off in your life. Similar is also the situation with rich and famous people who would buy a big farm just to be in competition with other's in the business. May be they are not able to afford a farm house but still we find that such persons buy the farm house with loan and lend up in paying higher interest amount with the bank just with the sole objective of show off to the persons in the same circle. Likewise, we also find that many persons show off with reference to purchase of a new car.

 Whether you need a new car or not but as soon as the new car enters the door of a neighbour, immediately you would like to buy out a new car just because the neighbour has a new car. Well, this type of show off activity can bring great financial constraint to you and once if you have a financial constraint in your day to day life, it will affect your health and definitely it will affect your happiness.

Hence, the best formula is never ever adopt the concept of show off. Rather, share your love with others. Let your love and affection to your friends and relatives just not be kept in your heart but express them your love and affection and that when you extend the love and affection flowing from your heart very liberally to your friends and relatives you find that your happiness increases ten times faster. So, just say today good bye to show off concept in your life.

36. Psychosomatic Diseases Can Be Cured for Your Health and Happiness

Psychosomatic diseases take away your health and once the health is in a bad shape, then you find no happiness in your life. But please do remember that psychosomatic diseases are curable. This is a reality. This is a fact and a statement which has now been accepted, approved and recognised even by the medical world. However, my personal feeling is that psychosomatic diseases can be removed in full just with the help of spiritual healing. If you believe in this concept, resort to spiritual healing and then you find that your psychosomatic diseases are surely going to be a thing of the past. Spiritual healing, I believe is a simple affair and that spiritual healing is not at all costly. It comes free of cost. Only the patient must have patience and the results are manifold. I have been thinking for a long time to carry out a research in the field of spiritual healing. The first and the foremost theme of spiritual healing is that the patient must have a faith in the concept of spiritual healing and the faith comes if you start reading the actual life stories of all those persons who have been benefited as a result of spiritual healing. I have read many such life stories and that is the reason I am convinced that spiritual healing can cure your psychosomatic diseases. I remember having read one small book containing the bio-data and the life time achievement of top 100 women of the world. In this book one story of a young lady who was feeling very broken but just as a result of spiritual healing she gained her strength. She gained her power. She gained her stamina and ultimately she gained a good health just because of spiritual healing. Spiritual healing demands a faith in the kingdom of Almighty God and once you have faith in the kingdom of God and you feel that God is there to help you, surely half of your psychosomatic will disappear instantly. Once this young lady when she got recovered, she started preaching and practising spiritual healing and nearly hundred years ago she was charging Dollar 100 as her professional fee. Her advice was having a great impact on the life of persons who met her because she had herself found a spiritual healing formula a super success which inspired her to regain her faith in health, to regain and experience the bliss of life only because of spiritual healing.

If you want to cure your psychosomatic disease, one option is to consult a doctor, take medicine and under influence of medicine please be happy. But this is not the long term permanent solution. The permanent solution lies within you. Have faith in this concept that my permanent solution is with me and that I will be able to cure myself of all my diseases with the power of God. Think of God as many times as you can during the day. Do have faith in the kingdom of God. This alone will be possible for doing away of majority of your psychosomatic problems.

All those who are having psychosomatic diseases should be in the company of such persons who are thinking positive in life. If you are surrounded in the company of such persons who are thinking negativity only, then your own personality also becomes negative. Hence, to achieve the best, have faith in God with spiritual healing which is without any medicine, without any side effect, without any other problem, you are able to overcome psychosomatic diseases which results into better health for you and ultimately better happiness in your life.

37. Your Happiness Formula: Worry Not for All That Has Not Happened

One of the important formulas for happiness is never ever to worry for all that has not happened. In your day to day life also you will find a large number of persons who are worried, who are tensed, who lose their appetite, who lose their health just because they are worried and worrying for all that which has not yet happened. Unnecessary worrying about an activity can take place at any age group.

Generally, during the opening of new school season we find a great big worry in the minds of all those mothers who are going to send their children for the first time to the school. They are worried and they are tensed.

They are not sure whether the child will get admission to the desired school. This worry many a time results into a big migraine headache for them and loss of their appetite. They consult the doctor, take the medicine but just by taking these medicines the answer is not permanent because this migraine and this loss of appetite has happened because of unnecessary worry about the admission of the child to the school. Supposing, you are in that situation, when your child is to be admitted to a new school, at that point of time just adopt action plan, work hard, try not in one but more than one school namely submit multiple admission forms in different schools.

Well, when we have a look at such persons who are facing this type of problem, we find that their face is becoming gloomy and the very thought of not getting the child admitted to the school, scares them. They are not interested to listen to this fact of no admission in the school for their young bright child.

Well, for every parent their child is definitely the brightest of all but still the admission is admission.

One may get and one may not get in a particular school. Well, at such point of time if you want to have your bliss of life and you do not want to lose your happiness, then never ever at any point of time worry for all that has not happened. You should only concentrate in doing the best in the given circumstances and then forget the rest. This is really the best happiness formula you can ever think of.

If you live this worldly life always with fear and always being worried about many facets of life and many activities which actually have not happened but which might have happened and the very thought of happening or non-happening of a particular event makes you worried.

Well, avoid such type of situation to make you happy and relaxed. Likewise, those in business, we find they are worried for the expected income they are to raise to meet office and residence. Well, the number of persons worrying on this account in whole India would be not less than 50 lakhs from India but in fact the income tax raid takes place on couple of thousand persons in a year only.

Still we find big quantity of persons who are worried and tensed about the income tax raid which might takes place at their residence. This worry and thought of suffering which has not happened is going to take away your robust health, make you ill, put you into depression.

Hence, the best answer is never ever to worry for all that which has really not happened. I remember the other day one young couple was having a boat drive. Both of them were very happy to enjoy this boat drive which was in a very big lake.

Suddenly while having the boat drive, in the mind of

the wife came a thought as to what will happen if by chance the boat were to be drowned as that she did not know swimming and she might die instantly. But her husband she knew knows swimming.

She went on to think that if this happens, then whether her husband will remarry another lady and if he is going to remarry, then whether he will forget me and what type of girl he will like to remarry and which type of girl he will get in remarriage and finally what will happen to her jewellery, who will get it? The new lady.

Well, these thoughts coming to the mind of this lady made dent in her happiness and she was unhappy for a long time.

Only when she spoke out all these things to her doctor, the doctor advised her to be calm and cool and never ever to worry for all those things which have never taken place.

Sometimes we also start worrying about what will happen after my death. This is a common question for which you are not able to talk to most of the people in the world. You are not able to talk on this question to your spouse, not with your children and not at all with your friends and relatives.

But the question that comes in your mind again and again is what will happen after I die. Your problem crops up in the mind when you have a look at your various assets, your houses, your cars, your businesses, your bank FDR and your jewelry.

Immediately you think that oh whole of my life I have been wasting my life only collecting all these precious assets but one day all these things I will have to give away and that you think in yet another moment that well you do not want to give everything but still the reality is you will have to give and this thought itself disturbs your mind.

You are now dead. Your mind is polluted. Your nervousness increases. Your health goes in the back gear and your happiness is vanished.

All these have happened only because of one single reason and that reason is that you have started worrying unnecessarily. Hence, to all my readers without any exception I will like them to adopt this simple formula of never to worry at all specially about those events and activities which have not taken place. Why should you at all worry about such situations and circumstances which have not taken place till now. Well, develop this attitude and then you find happiness and happiness all round.

Those in business adopt greatly the theme of getting worried and tensed about the host of various activities which might not have taken place.

For example one gentleman supplies big quantity of goods to a new customer and the next day he was worried and tensed because he was worried on the account of whether the amount will be recovered or not from that new buyer and it is this worry which gets him on his toes and his creativity gets lost.

Therefore, never ever worry about all that has not happened. Similarly, I have found many exporters going to China from India, many importers going to China and making big imports. They are making money. They have found a good market in China. They have found the cheapest source of purchase from China and that they are able to sell in India the goods which they bring and finally make their money.

But the problem is if such person starts worrying and thinking what will happen if some 400 people were to go to China and import the same item and sell it at a lower price, then their business could just collapse in one single day. This type of thinking is known as negative thinking and thus, one should always avoid thinking about all that has not yet happened in your life.

If you adopt this formula in all spheres of your life whether social, family or business, then you will find that worry and tension are less in your life, creativity is more and happiness definitely is more because your mind is not disturbed or distracted by thinking about all that which has not happened in your life.

38. Timely Legal Compliances Keep You Happy

Legal compliances make a lot of tension, worry and they can also give you lot of strain and stress in your day to day life. The best formula is to always comply with legal formalities within time. Never keep last day as your fulfillment of obligation date for any legal compliance to be made by you. Always make your compliances in time and once you make all your legal compliances in time, then you find that you are a happy person. If this formula is implemented in action then stress, tension and the worries are not on your neck. Therefore, best formula will be to prepare yearly chart of your various legal obligations and start complying with these obligations from time to time. If you work in a haphazard manner and you do not comply with the legal formalities in time, then it is possible that noncompliance of certain legal matters can take away your happiness because such noncompliance at your end of these legal issues may in many cases result into payment of penal interest as well as payment of penalty and in some cases noncompliance of statutory provisions may even mean your prosecution in life. Hence, it is time for you now to always think of legal compliance in time to avoid all the worry and all the tensions of your life. A legal compliance if complied on a regular basis makes you tension free and does not bring your problem in your head. Whatever you are to comply with, whatever statutory payments you have to do and whatever statutory returns have to be filed by you if they are all kept, recorded on a piece of paper then your life is easy and simple. Then you have no worry, no tension and no stress at all. Such a person enjoys better happiness in life. Reversely, if you are a person who does not comply to legal compliances regularly, only at the last moment when you come to know of your obligation, you start making the payment or you file the tax return and you accuse the Accounts Department or you accuse your Legal Department or you accuse the manager but the fact is it has been purely your own mistake of noncompliance because you have never had kept the compliance charts handy and ready. It is time now for those specially in business to prepare a compliance chart and let that compliance chart be monitored by you on a regular basis. If it is monitored on a regular basis, then surely the chances are that you will have all your legal compliances committed and fulfilled on time which reduces your stress level and once the stress is less, then surely happiness is more. Therefore, please comply with the legal formalities including filing of the income-tax returns, filing of other statutory returns, compliance of the Registrar of Companies formalities, payments of Provident Fund, payments relating to service tax and other payments which you are required to make during the course of your business. Similarly, if any legal notice is received by you, always act fast on the same, take the legal notice carefully and do not just avoid complying the legal notice. You may think you are correct and therefore you do not comply at all to the legal notice. Well, that is not correct. Even if you are right which you feel but still let there will be compliance to the legal notice, let there be compliance with summon if received by you and thus if you are able to comply regularly all the legal formalities, you find that your life is full of peace and happiness.

39. WAP: Another Happiness Formula

If you want to be happy, then always adopt WAP formula. I have implemented this WAP formula for a large number of my clients, business associates and friends and have found that this WAP formula really does wonders for achieving your happiness. Well, the WAP formula means—Work Action Plan. This WAP formula implies that whenever you are tensed, whenever you are worried, whenever you have got pressure of work, it is at that point of time that you should try to prepare your "Work Action Plan" which will enable you in a guaranteed manner to control your worries and tensions. No doubt it is true that if your worried and tensions are kept under control, then it is possible for you to achieve higher results in happiness.

One should always prepare a daily agenda or weekly agenda and a quarterly agenda so that one can plan his or her affairs keeping in view the pressure of work and the agenda items. Work Action Plan that is WAP really helps you in zeroing down the level of your stress specially relating to the work with which you are concerned. Hence, whenever there is pressure of work, it is time for you to plan your WAP and then start acting on it fast so that you are able to achieve better happiness for you.

My research brings in a conclusion that anxiety and stress levels can surely come under control only when work action plan (WAP) activated is set to roll in full action.

The modern medicines claim to control anxiety coupled with stress under control by constant and regular use of these modern medicines. But, the fact remains that medicines cannot bring out a complete 100% sure success answer to your day to day anxiety and stress. However, if such a stressed person shifts to WAP activity namely Work Action Plan then surely he will be able to control anxiety as also stress even without a regular dose of medicines. But believe in this dictum and see for your own self a complete relief from anxiety and stress just by your faith in implementing this concept of — Work Action Plan (WAP).

Do remember that WAP is not just one time activity to bring results in controlling your anxiety and stress but the fact is that it is a way of life to be followed on a regular basis and then you find that your anxiety and stress would be a thing of the past.

The WAP concept is not just for rich and famous persons engaged in business or profession but this WAP formula is equally profitable for creative use by home makers in their day to day life. The modern housewife has a lot more work these days in comparison to the old time. The new age ladies are called upon to work for better economic welfare of the family and that she has also to take care of the home front. At times the house wife might get a severe blow to her health due to work stress at office and home front which may produce anxiety but it can be controlled in a real practical manner with this WAP formula.

This WAP formula can also help students to control their study related worries and tensions as a student can also effectively overcome his problems through WAP.

Your WAP (Work Action Plan) would surely help you to increase the happiness level in your life.

40. Time to Buy Your Happiness

Well, you may be surprised or astonished to hear this statement that yes you can buy your happiness. Questions may arise in your mind which is that super store where happiness is available for sale. Don't worry. The answer is that this happiness store lies in every town and in every road of India and the world. It is your desire to buy your happiness which ultimately can genuinely result into increase in your happiness. If you want to try, try out the simple formula of buying your happiness. Well, the buying activity of happiness is not a costly affair. It can be implemented with as low as 50 or 100 rupees and the higher happiness you want, then higher dose of money is required to buy out your happiness.

To start with simple formula, just buy one blanket by spending only Rs.100. Now, once you have purchased the blanket, it is time for you now to give away this blanket to someone who is poor, someone who is needy. The next step is to identify such a person who is really needy and who deserves a blanket and such a person you have to identify now who cannot even afford 100 rupees to buy one single blanket. Once you identify such a person, now please give away with your folded hand this blanket which you have purchased for Rs.100. Now, start the programme of encashing upon your happiness which you have derived as a result of spending some money. Just implement it and then experience for yourself the happiness coming to your doorstep as a result of buying happiness in the form of purchasing some article or thing and then giving away to the poor and the needy. The other day myself and my son Satyapriya went to Sadar Bazar area in Delhi. This is a very big wholesale market and from this market we purchased at least 10 to 15 big jars of toffees and chocolates. The next day we went to two schools in Greater Kailash II area and distributed these chocolates and toffees to the students studying in these small schools. This small little activity which might have cost us hardly Rs. 2000 provided us immense happiness and pleasure. When we entered the school, first of all we asked the children whether they would like to have one toffee or two toffees. Naturally most of the children would say two toffees. But finally we told them that look today we are not going to give you two toffees but just bring your hand inside this jar and take with your one hand as many toffees as you can lift at one go. Some of the children got scared. They have never seen such a type of thing happened in the past. Some of them were perplexed. But we found great happiness when we could see the children's faces which became very happy and which were full of enthusiasm when they lifted a big bowl of chocolates and toffees in their hands from this jar which we had taken to their school. One of the student of Class V took out the maximum number of toffees. His count was 37 toffees in one go. This small little activity speaks that yes we can buy happiness. I want my readers also to spend some small little time and spend little money and distribute some of these items to the poor and the needy and experience for yourself the bliss and happiness. Similar would be the situation if you go to a weekly bazaar in your neighbourhood. Generally, in this weekly bazaar generally the persons below the poverty line and persons of class IV staff type generally go to purchase their weekly needs. If you want happiness then visit just one of this type of bazaar and then buy out a small little toy or a small little dress for someone who is really very poor and cannot afford the dress. If you extend a small little courtesy of this type then you find that your happiness is going to go up in a guaranteed manner.

41. Chant and Be Happy

One of the very important and practical happiness formula is to chant. What to chant is the million dollar question which might be coming up in the minds of our readers. Well, the simple and the plain answer is chant any name of the Almighty God on which you have faith. Do remember that chanting has got the capacity to provide you happiness on the one hand while on the other hand chanting has also the capacity to remove your worries and tensions. Thus, it is time now for you to adopt chanting as a part of your daily routine. Just like every morning you get up and you have a cup of tea and then the breakfast followed by lunch and thereafter the dinner. Similarly, make it a habit to chant the name of the Almighty God every day without any lapse on your part. If you just adopt this simple formula, then surely you will have happiness at your side with you and always with you. If you have never had any experience of chanting, then it is worthwhile to discuss the different vistas or different themes of chanting the name of the Almighty God. The first type of chanting or japa is known as Baikhari Jap or Vachika Jap. This Vachika Jap of chanting is the way of chanting whereby you repeat the name of the Almighty as loudly as possible and this system of chanting is most suitable for all those persons who are adopting chanting for the first time. Hence, for beginners who have never had the occasion to experience the magic of chanting in their life, for them this Vachika Jap is strongly recommended. Your brain gets charged with the powerful vibrations of the mantra which you are chanting. Hence, keep your eyes open and continue to chant any one name of the Almighty God or anyone mantra. If you are in a fix and you are not sure what to chant, then simply start chanting Om. Om chanting has got the powerful effect of providing happiness to you and also cleaning your body and mind.

Another way of chanting is known as Upanshu Jap or Upanshu Chanting. In this concept of chanting you should not speak the mantra or the name of God in a loud manner. Rather, while you are chanting the name of God, just chant by whispering the name of the God or the mantra. Thus, under Upanshu concept only lips are moved and there is no loud or external sound while you are chanting. For best results have half eyes open and half eyes closed while you are continuing your Upanshu chanting. The third type of chanting is known as Manasik Jap or Manasik chanting. In this concept of chanting no sound at all is uttered and the lips also do not move. Thus, under Manasik Jap or Manasik Chanting the mantra or the name of the God is not repeated loudly nor it is whispered. The person chanting only utters the name of the Almighty God or the mantra while closing the lips and making no noise at all. Under Manasik Jap concept it is better to close the eyes so as to experience better quality of jap or chanting for you.

The last category of chanting is known as Likhit Jap or Likhit Chanting in which concept you are required to go on writing the mantra or the name of the Almighty God hundreds of time. While you are writing, you are also repeating the name of the mantra or the name of the Almighty God without uttering a single word from your lips. Thus, lips are closed, noise is not made, the mantra or the name of the God is written by you with your hand while the name continues to be recited inner and inner side only. Thus, you write the name of the God or mantra and recite the same internally that is known as the Likhit Jap.

Out of the various types of Japas or chanting mentioned above which one appears to be the best, may be the question that is posed and that is coming to the mind of our readers. Well, the fact remains that chanting in any manner will have the same purpose and the same impact on your mind and body. However, what remains to be seen and to be followed is that whatever system of chanting makes you comfortable, just adopt the same system of chanting for you. Do not copy others.

Let others continue chanting in the manner they like. But let your chanting be done in the manner in which you feel comfortable. At any point of time when drowsiness is at bay, you feel something like depressed, sometimes you are angry, sometimes you are unhappy, at all these real life situations in life, it is time now for you to just chant and be happy.

ISKCON the Hare Ram Hare Krishna Temple people adopt chanting in a very meticulous manner. Their whole concept of providing peace to the humanity in this worldly life is in the concept of chanting alone.

I had the rare privilege of personally meeting and listening to the chanting sessions with the Founder of ISKCON temple. I still remember it was sometime in July 1970 while I was in New York, I found Swami Prabhupadji, the Founder of the ISKCON chanting on the famous Fifth Avenue of New York City.

From that time I myself felt inspired by this great concept of chanting which plays a very major role in your life to provide you happiness at all time. Besides, chanting also increases concentration which ultimately helps you to perform better in your student life or in your business or professional life as well. I also strongly believe that chanting of "Om" helps in concentration specially when Om is uttered, we find that a sort of effort moves from our throat to the brain and this activity assists in the concentration of the mind. Hence, adopt chanting and more particularly adopt "Om" chanting for your concentration of mind.

Do remember that if your mind is concentrated, it will help you in your process of happiness. A research study conducted by various foreign universities have brought conclusion that "Om" chanting can bring calmness of the mind.

Make chanting a habit of your life, a part of your daily routine and just then only start experiencing for yourself the real bliss and the happiness which also will become a part of your own life.

42. Fear Not for Your Own Health and Happiness

Fear is such illness that has got the greatest capacity at one go to take away your health and happiness. Hence, never let fear enter your mind and body. Do remember that if fear enters your brain, then it will in the first place have a very negative effect on your health and it is a fact that if health is not well, then happiness cannot be achieved.

Whenever in this worldly life you experience the fear, the cause of the fear may be nothing special but fear is after all fear and just you experience that fear, at that point of time, it is time for you to think and think and meditate the reasons for such fear and the outcome of that fear.

Ten to fifteen minutes thinking on this topic and theme will convince you in a guaranteed manner that merely worrying now about the fear and having anxiety about the fear will not bring any peace to you.

Reversely, it will help in the process of downgrading your robust health and once the health is on the wrong track, the happiness obviously going to follow the foot steps of your bad health.

At least keeping this view in mind, it is time for you now and never to worry at all. The worries in life should be handled in a positive manner and one way to fight the fear is to think of inner silence.

The inner silence can be practiced by you by closing your eyes and becoming aware of the body and experiencing the sensation of touch of the body and being aware of the external sounds and also becoming aware of your breath and later on forgetting the outer sounds and just concentrating on your breath, this type of activity helps you to let go off fear.

Sit calmly and repeat that I will keep my mind free and I will not at all allow my fear to conquer my mind. Also think that my mind is the king. Fear cannot take the seat of king of myself. This type of thinking will definitely help you in letting go of the fear from your life zone.

43. How to Be Happy under Unhappy Circumstances and Situations of Life

Most of the readers would think that why are we going to discuss non practical pointers in this book. Well, for most of you, you will find it difficult to be happy specially in unhappy circumstances and situations. I am no exception to this reality of life faced by most of us. But the fact remains that my father Shri R.N. Lakhotia's way of life leads me to think and believe the fact that we can be happy even under unhappy circumstances and situations. Those who come in contact with my father have always experienced that he is the living example of spreading and providing happiness to one and all who meet him and this is mainly because he is always happy even in circumstances where under normal condition a person would be unhappy. Friends believe me when I say that it is your attitude of life that makes your thinking to be happy or unhappy. Hence, whether there are situations or whether there are circumstances and whether they are created by you or not but still you have the right to be happy in all situations and in all circumstances. Hence, try to absorb the thinking that be happy even under unhappy circumstances and situations. It is not impossible. It can only be a difficult situation. But just try to adopt this way of life to help you achieve the best of you in your life and thus make you happy in all situations and at all times.

44. Superior Happiness

One of the important aim of this life is to achieve happiness. Entire humanity in this new millennium is looking forward to achieving happiness at any cost and by any means. A step ahead of happiness is known as "Superior Happiness." The real joy or bliss of Superior Happiness cannot be described in words but can be only experienced.

To achieve Superior Happiness it does not cost too much money. It is rather the intense desire for experiencing Superior Happiness which alone brings it.

The basic grass root concept of achieving Superior Happiness lies in leading a real simple life, without much show and also by having control of all your desires.

It is not the riches of the world which can guarantee Superior Happiness in this worldly life. Long ago Socrates said that Men are to be esteemed for their virtue, not their wealth. He further said, that "Fine and rich clothes are suited for comedians." The wicked live to eat, the good eat to be able to live. Persons desiring Superior Happiness must lead a simple life and must work hard in order to avoid idleness for it said that the idle life makes an easy target for the devil.

Thomas Aquinas had declared that it is impossible for happiness, which is the ultimate aim of men, to consist in wealth and that true happiness can be attained through the vision of divine essence. Sharing one's excess "riches" with the poor is one of the ways of enjoying and experiencing the Superior Happiness. This is the view of great philosopher Calvin who felt that attainment of wealth was the sign of God's blessing.

Persons desiring Superior Happiness should not make

vulgar display of their assets and possessions. It may be interesting to note that way back in the year 1651 the members of Massachusetts General Court had issued sumptuary decree stating that "no person whose visible estates shall not exceed the true and indifferent value of 200 pounds shall wear any Gold, or silver, or silver lace, or Gold & Silver buttons, or any bone lace above 2 shillings per yard, or silk hoods or scarves, the penalty of 10 shillings for every such offence shall be levied." It appears that with such stringent rules and regulations which existed over 300 years ago then at that time the quality of life would have been better in those years and during that era superior happiness would have been a reality for most of the civilians.

Transcendental simplicity is yet another avenue to achieve Superior Happiness since transcendentalists are of the view that the human life is too precious to waste on mere pursuit and enjoyment of things and the common goal of the followers of transcendental simplicity principles was to develop such modes of living that reduced their material and institutional needs to minimum extent so that a person could easily pursue spiritual truths and moral ideals. Thus, the follower of transcendental simplicity is bound to achieve "Superior Happiness" as he would be less attached to the worldly pursuits. Emerson and Thoreau believed in the concept of transcendental simplicity.

Emerson believed in the romantic desire to pursue simplicity. Thus simple living is the passport for superior happiness and bliss. Thoreau was fundamentally preacher of the theme—"simplify your life."

With the increase in the possessions of a person, his desires do increase and then the person is required to work harder, worry more and communicate less with his family and friends, says an article printed in New York Times of

11th November, 1904. Hence, all those desiring Superior Happiness should remove from their mind the only aim of increasing riches at any cost in any manner.

Roosevelt had once declared that excessive materialism was the greatest danger threatening the country. Even in this new millennium this is true. Edward Bok the Editor of Ladies Home Journal wrote that it was hard thing for those who have little to believe that the greatest happiness of life is with them: that it is not with those who have abundance. He went on to say that "more we have the less we actually enjoy it." Bok further went to say that the woman of simplest means is the happiest woman on earth, if she only knew it. Thus, specially for ladies the Superior Happiness would lie in keep means to its minimum. David Grayson attributed the "habit of contentment" which provided him happiness. Yes, in true sense it is contentment which brings in "Superior Happiness" for all human beings.

Ralph Borsodi a social critic of New York in the late 1920s was of the view that when a person produces more things that are necessary to good living, he wastes the time and the material both of which should be used to make the world a more beautiful place to live. He practiced the theme of creative pleasure and felt that rural and simple life would bring spiritual satisfaction.

More and more people the world over are now sick and tired of the present day complicated life and yearn for superior happiness which can be achieved by augmenting simple life style and by enjoying the joys of contact with nature. Way back seventy five years ago Edward Bob in USA expressed the feelings of the people as "Money is King" and "Business is our God commerce rules." But when he was 56 years old as well as wealthy he was controlling the famous Ladies Home Journal which in the year 1919 was selling 20,00,000 copies, still he left his business and decided to devote his money to philanthropy while his time to social service. I think that moulding his life in this manner must have brought him superior happiness. He advocated early retirement and was of the view that "bliss in possession does not last." The real bliss of life lies in aiming to achieve superior happiness.

Way back in the year 1920 Lewis Muneford charged that "How many men sweat in their offices so that they may give their wives a private car, a house with multiple bath rooms, or expensive furs." While dealing with the concept of happiness he said that how many men whose wives could be far more happy, far more richly satisfied, with a little more of their husbands time and a little more of lover's attentions. His advice to the community at large was that to achieve simplicity and happiness strip away needless superfluities, try to make work more satisfying and less stifling, concentrate on developing more sincere personal and family relations and finally strive to reach the synthesis of practicability and spirituality. Well, these are also the end targets of achieving superior happiness.

For those desiring to achieve superior happiness and the bliss of happiness should adopt gentleness, frugality, humility and simplicity which will ultimately mean plain living, high thinking and the higher real Superior Happiness.

45. Social Networking Sites for Your Happiness

Lonely you feel. Why just you. Most of your friends even if they are having a big circle of their friends, still feel lonely at many intervals in life. The best answer is to get a social networking site which will provide happiness for you. Definitely crores of people in the whole world have gained their happiness by visiting social networking sites. I find specially the youth of the world getting crazy for the social networking site. Specially it provides happiness to them and that is the reason why the youth in particular is spending substantial quality time in being linked with the social networking cite. I feel that mainly this activity will be responsible for providing happiness to you. Facebook is one such networking site which has been instrumental not merely in India but in the world over in providing happiness to crores of people. In the same manner certain chat sites can also help you in providing happiness. Some of the chat sites as sent to me by my friend are as under:

1. VZones - http://www.vzones.com
2. Talk City - http://www.talkcity.com
3. Active Chat Rooms - http://www.active-chat-rooms.biz/top-chat
4. Worlds.com - http://www.world.net
5. Spinchat - http://www.spin-chat.com
6. gotowebcams- http://www.gotowebcams.com
7. Yahoo Chat - http://chat.yahoo.com
8. AOL Instant Messenger - http://www.aim.com
9. icq - http://web.icq.com

10. Msn Messenger - http://www.msnmessenger-download.com
   Source:www.toptensites.com

My friend has mentioned to me that his regular visit to these websites have seen to gain for him the lost happiness. May be you may also find your happiness hidden in these websites or social networking or in the chat sites.

46. Snatching an Hour a Day Can Make You Happy

Reframe, reorganise, readjust your own daily agenda and your activities chart with the aim of finding an hour a day for you. We have known the fact that an apple a day keeps the doctor away. In the same manner if you are able to snatch an hour a day from your daily routine, then surely it is possible for you to get more happiness, better happiness, quality happiness for you. We have read long ago that if you lose an hour a day, we go on searching it for the whole day. Hence, adjust, realign, rethink but in any case by whatsoever reason try to find out an hour a day extra for you. If you are able to find an hour a day for you, then surely it will be a milestone in setting up your happiness formula. The best way in a guaranteed manner to snatch an hour a day is to get up just an hour early from whatsoever time you are getting up from in your normal schedule. The advantage is if you are able to get an hour for you, you feel happy, you feel satisfied, you find sometime available in your life for yourself and it gives you happiness because in this one special hour you are able to do anything what you like. So, act now. Plan your agenda. Write your priority in life. Write your main activities to be done. Plan start right now for different activities of day but end of the day try to find an hour for you. This hour found out by you will be your exclusive happiness formula.

47. MCP Programme for Health and Happiness

Well, MCP would be a wonderful programme to bring health and happiness for you and again this MCP Programme can be implemented by anyone at any time in your life. Let MCP be a part of your day to day routine. If you make this MCP as a part of your regular habit, your health and happiness definitely is going to increase. Well, your next question will be what after all is this MCP? MCP stands for a programme comprising of meditation—chanting—prayer. I want you to adopt a theme of meditation at least for sometime of the day in your life. There is no requirement of any fixed timing for getting out your meditation activity. Similarly, there is also no requirement that while you meditate, you must sit at the same place on all the days. Also please do remember that there is no requirement that you should have a bath and then start your meditation. The life has been made very, very simple for us specially when it comes to meditation. You can meditate at any point of time at any place in any situation. However, the best meditation practice would be to start your meditation in the morning. When you start meditation, surely early morning is the best because if you meditate in the early hours of the morning, the power of meditation would increase and the result would be provide you better health and happiness at least 25% more if you carry out meditation activities early in the morning. If you like, you can sit down and carry out your meditation activity. Sit calmly and coolly on your bed and you can continue meditation. If you like, you nay close your eyes or you may keep the eyes open while carrying out meditation. The impact however, remains the same. Some top religious organisations of the world believe in carrying out meditation with eyes open. However, many other organisations when they talk of meditation, they are of the view that meditation should be done with closed eyes. Scientific research has revealed that it is immaterial with reference to the impact of benefit of a meditation whether the same is carried out with closed eyes or with open eyes. Similarly, meditation may also be done in a sitting posture or may be conducted in the sleeping posture. Likewise, meditation may be conducted in your room or sitting your office or sitting in the car also or sitting in the bus or a metro train. Hence, meditation is not a time bound programme. It is only regularity wise top programme for which if regularity maintained, it results into higher level of happiness and health for you alone.

Many times we find persons stating that while they are meditating, they are not able to concentrate. They don't know how to meditate. Well to start your meditation, start with one name of God. Which name of the God should I repeat? This may be your next question. Well, the correct answer is repeat any name of the God which you like. And start repeating the name of God while you close your eyes and meditate. I personally am of the view that closing the eyes and meditating brings in better results and better concentration. Your meditation helps you to increase your power of concentration which indirectly helps in better health for you and ultimately provides happiness for day long. Hence, please carry out meditation activity on a regular basis.

Chanting is equally very important, specially for your health. Do remember that if health gets improved as a result of chanting, your happiness will be a pursuit of the same. The question is at what point to do chanting and for how long to carry out chanting and then another question that might come in the mind is what should we chant. Well, one can carry out chanting at any point of time. You can do chanting in the morning, in the afternoon, in the night or before going to bed. The best formula I would like to recommend is to do chanting early in the morning backed by closing day chanting to be performed just five minutes before going to bed. If you adopt this formula of chanting particularly at the close of the day while you retire for the day, then surely you will have a great wonderful, undisturbed sleep which will bring better health for you. Try this and experience for yourself the bliss of chanting. Those who are new to the concept of resorting to chanting may also find a question cropping up in their mind relating to the time period for which one should do chanting. Well, there is no specified time limit which can be said to be the most appropriate one for your health and happiness but I feel that one should start chanting for 5 minutes per day and try to increase the quantum of your chanting to 10, 20 or 30 minutes in a day. The fact however, remains that the more you do adopt chanting, the more concentrated your mind becomes and more the chanting, the more active mind becomes and more the chanting, the more vibrant the mind becomes. Now, that the question is answered immediately by yourself and that is how strong you want your mind to be.

Accordingly, plan your strategy for adopting the chanting programme in your day to day life. What I would like to recommend is that it is not the period for which you are chanting that is important but it is the regular habit of your chanting which will bring its results for you instantly. If you are busy, you are not able to do chanting in the morning. But at least you can all adopt a formula of chanting while you retire for the day. Just 5 to 10 minutes before going to bed start chanting and then you find that your worries and tensions are a thing of the past and while going to bed your mind lies in real tense free situation and your mind is really relaxed. Also do remember that your mind is relaxed. It helps in your getting better sleep which is a prerequisite for your good health. Another question that might crop up in the minds of the readers is what do I chant. The answer is chant anything. Chant any holy mantra whichever is clear to you. The importance of chanting lies in just chanting and not the particular name for which chanting has to be done. Hence, just adopt any name of the God and start your chanting activity right now for your own health and your happiness. By chance you are not able to find any good mantra or any good phrase which you should adopt while chanting, then please chant Om. In case you are not able to concentrate on chanting then switch on your music system with a CD or a Cassette of any Mantra and continue your chanting with it.

Prayer to the God develops your inner strength. Prayers offered to God help you in accepting the real facts of life. At least there is someone to whom you can talk freely and that someone is your own Almighty God. To achieve the best results for health and happiness to be derived from prayers, one must pray in the morning just after taking bath and getting ready, pray for a few minutes before staring your day to day routine activity and again end the day by offering prayers to the Almighty God and thanking God for all that He has done for you today. If you adopt this simple formula of offering prayer to the Almighty God in the morning as well as in the evening, then surely you will find your heart becomes very light. You experience happiness and better health all day round. Hence, start offering prayers to the Almighty God at least twice a day. Some of the persons think that offering one or two hours a prayer is going to be better for them and will result into better health and happiness. Well this is your own thinking.

But what I personally feel and believe is that it is not the quantum of time spent in prayers which is your health and happiness but what is important is the quality of prayers which alone is important for your health and happiness. A person may spend one hour or two hours every day in prayer and at the time of extending prayers for an hour or two whenever the mobile phone rings, he receives the phone in between also. If we compare another person who just offers prayers for five minutes only but while he is praying to God he is extending concentrated prayer with no obstacles to come in between. I strongly feel that a small duration of prayer is better than prayer at a long time without focus concentration. Hence, carry out your prayer regularly may be for a short duration but whenever you are doing prayer do remember while offering prayers you are just concentrating on prayer and at the same time nothing is there.

I strongly believe that if prayer becomes a part of your daily routine life. Then the real happiness would be at your door step.

48. Live in Today for Your Happiness

Think not of the gone yesterday. Think not of the tomorrow to come but just think in the present. Well, this is my happiness formula which I prescribe to one and all who come in my contact in various seminars and talk shows in different parts of India. This simple theme has helped to gain happiness in a large group of people specially when I tell them that they should think only on what they are today. It is only just that point which they should think, again think, ponder and finally derive happiness..

It is time for you now to thank the Almighty God for all that He has given you. It is also time right now to have a stop thinking of all that is not with you. Whether it is your business, your physical possessions of gold, jewellery and assets or it is the family in all situations just concentrate on what you have today. Enjoy all that is with you today and then you are a happy man. If you start thinking about what you could have had or what you had in the past but that you are not possessing all that what you had in the past, thinking on these lines brings negativity in the mind which causes unhappiness for you. Hence, time now is to just think on the theme of living in today and this formula alone makes you happy.

When we talk of thinking about living in today that is in the present day time, my emphasis is to think today on all the aspects of living today. If you want to be happy while you are living in today, think about the material wealth you have got right now. Likewise, thinking on the family front also it is time for you now to think only about all the family members which are existing right now in your family. Hence, do not think of all those who were part of your family and who have left today. Those family members who have gone, who are not with you today, just thinking on that line alone may make you unhappily and may bring you unhappiness in your life. But just think only about the family members who are with you today. This type of thinking will shower happiness in your life. Similarly, do not sit down and think of what will happen in future when some of the family members would die. How will you face the situation then ? Never ever let your mind to think on these types of silly situations. Rather, be positive. Think only on one point and that is as on today what is the state of affairs of my family, of my wealth, of my recognition in this society etc., etc. If you develop this habit of living in the present, thinking in the present, then your happiness continues to be in the present form. Reversely, on any aspect of life, if you start thinking about the gone old times, then you yourself enters the door of the old time and that may be the cause of your unhappiness. I remember one gentleman coming from a very rich zamindar family of West Bengal used to always think only about the number of buildings which they were having 50 years ago. He would recollect that 50 years ago there were some 12 to 14 big houses in the names of their family members in Kolkata alone, they also had lot of agricultural land but today they are just having two houses only. When he thinks about this, he feels unhappy. He feels cheers not entering his life. Well, such a person could be happy if he were to be contended with thinking that today at least I have got two houses and then proceeds to thank the Almighty God for the fact that even today there are two houses. Similarly, another gentleman lost his mother about five years back. He is always thinking and remembering that his mother is no more with him. He is always in a gloomy mood. After all the fact was that he has great attachment with his mother. But when he met me, I told him and inspired him to live in today only. Last week when

I met him again, I found that he has completely transformed. He is very happy person. Now, he is happy all the time and the vibrations of his happiness can be seen from his face itself. The simple reason now of his happiness is that he is happy, just thinking only about all the family members which are existing as on today. He feels happy that his father is alive. He feels happy when he finds that he has a wife, a son, a daughter-in-law, two grand children and one brother. He feels happy when he finds that has a sister, a brother-in-law and grand children. He will definitely continue to miss his mother but the fact is that the happiness is possible in his life only because he is living and thinking in today. If you want to be happy, always live in today and think today and then happy person you are.

The other day I met a businessman who Is having now a very small business of running a travel agency in Mumbai. I used to know this gentleman who was my client five decades ago. Today coming from a famous family of industrialists, this young man feels unhappy all the time because in his mind memory lane reflects a sense of a big factory which was being run by his father and grand father and where about 4000 workers were employed, it was a big textile mill. Today the mill is not there. The bank liabilities have taken away the mill, the land and all the assets of the family. Thinking of this old situation, thinking of this past, this gentleman is always unhappy. His unhappiness is instrumental also in his lower business productivity. When I met him during one of my flight to Mumbai, I told him to be happy in the present situation. Now the other day he telephoned me to say that his business of travel agency has been doubled. He has stopped talking and thinking about negativity. He has stopped thinking about a big factory which they had in their family and his only thinking today is with reference to his present day travel business. Now, as he is living in the present day, he is feeling happy and as he is happy, his business has grown by leaps and bounds and that is the reason this year his turnover and his profit is almost double in comparison with the preceding year.

My dear friend if you find at any point of life in your life that you are unhappy because you have been thinking about the glorious past of your family or you are thinking about the future glory which might take place in the family, then you will be unhappy always. But if you want to be happy, then enjoy what you have today. Enjoy the business. Enjoy the service which you are having today. Enjoy the family of yours as on today and enjoy the social life, the spiritual life, the cultural life which you are enjoying today and continue enjoying the fellowship and friendship of you friends, relatives, acquaintances and then you will find happiness, oh yes happiness is there with you always and for ever.

49. Inspiring Quotations on Happiness

Just read one "Happiness Quotation" a day, this will add to your Happiness. Also send me a Happiness Quotation dear to you so that I can incorporate it in my next edition of this book. Write to me at – Subhash Lakhotia, S-228, Greater Kailash Part-2, New Delhi-110048, Phone: 011-29215434, M. 09810001665

A table, a chair, a bowl of fruit and a violin; what else does a man need to be happy?

- Albert Einstein

Being happy is something you have to learn. I often surprise myself by saying "Wow, this is it. I guess I'm happy. I got a home I love. A career that I love. I'm even feeling more and more at peace with myself." If there's something else to happiness, let me know. I'm ambitious for that, too."

- Harrison Ford

Since you get more joy out of giving joy to others, you should put a good deal of thought into the happiness that you are able to give.

- Eleanor Roosevelt

Joy can be real only if people look upon their life as a service, and have a definite object in life outside themselves and their personal happiness.

- Leo Nikolaevich Tolstoy

The greatest degree of inner tranquility comes from the development of love and compassion. The more we care for the happiness of others, the greater is our own sense of well-being.

- Tenzin Gyatso, 14th Dalai Lama

Each morning when I open my eyes I say to myself: I, not events, have the power to make me happy or unhappy today. I can choose which it shall be. Yesterday is dead, tomorrow hasn't arrived yet. I have just one day, today, and I'm going to be happy in it.

- *Groucho Marx*

Hope is itself a species of happiness, and perhaps, the chief happiness which this world affords.

- *Samuel Johnson*

Knowledge of what is possible is the beginning of happiness.

- *George Santayana*

Person who travels on nothing from nowhere to happiness.

- *Mark Twain*

If you want to be happy, set a goal that commands your thoughts, liberates your energy, and inspires your hopes.

- *Andrew Carnegie*

Thousands of candles can be lighted from a single candle, and the life of the candle will not be shortened. Happiness never decreases by being shared.

- *Buddha*

Most people are about as happy as they make up their minds to be.

- *Abraham Lincoln*

The amount of happiness that you have depends on the amount of freedom you have in your heart.

- *Thich Nhat Hanh*

Everything is material for the seed of happiness, if you look into it with inquisitiveness and curiosity. The future is completely open, and we are writing it moment to moment. There always is the potential to create an environment of blame or one that is conducive to loving-kindness.

- Pema Chodron

It is a great mitzvah to be happy always.

- Rebbe Nachman of Breslov

There is neither happiness nor misery in the world; there is only the comparison of one state to another, nothing more. He who has felt the deepest grief is best able to experience supreme happiness. We must have felt what it is to die, that we may appreciate the enjoyments of life.

- Alexandre Dumas

Even a happy life cannot be without a measure of darkness, and the word happy would lose its meaning if it were not balanced by sadness. It is far better take things as they come along with patience and equanimity.

- Carl Jung

My life has no purpose, no direction, no aim, no meaning, and yet I'm happy. I can't figure it out. What am I doing right?

- Charles Schulz

Satisfaction of one's curiosity is one of the greatest sources of happiness in life.

- Linus Pauling

To be without some of the things you want is an indispensable part of happiness.

- Bertrand Russell

The modern fairy tale ending is the reverse of the traditional one: A woman does not wait for Prince Charming to bring her happiness; she lives happily ever after only by refusing to wait for him or by actually rejecting him. It is those who persist in hoping for a Prince Charming who are setting themselves up for disillusionment and unhappiness.

- Susan Faludi

It is an illusion that youth is happy, an illusion of those who have lost it.

- W. Somerset Maugham

One should never direct people towards happiness, because happiness too is an idol of the marketplace. One should direct them towards mutual affection. A beast gnawing at its prey can be happy too, but only human beings can feel affection for each other, and this is the highest achievement they can aspire to.

- Aleksandr Solzhenitsyn

People say that money is not the key to happiness, but I always figured if you have enough money, you can have a key made.

- Joan Rivers

All men have a sweetness in their life. That is what helps them go on. It is towards that they turn when they feel too worn out.

- Albert Camus

To forgive is the highest, most beautiful form of love. In return, you will receive untold peace and happiness.

- Robert Muller

What everyone wants from life is continuous and genuine happiness.

- Baruch Spinoza

Gratefulness is the key to a happy life that we hold in our hands, because if we are not grateful, then no matter how much we have we will not be happy because we will always want to have something else or something more.

- David Steindl-Rast

The basic thing is that everyone wants happiness, no one wants suffering. And happiness mainly comes from our own attitude, rather than from external factors. If your own mental attitude is correct, even if you remain in a hostile atmosphere, you feel happy.

- Tenzin Gyatso, 14th Dalai Lama

But what is happiness except the simple harmony between a man and the life he leads?

- Albert Camus

Happiness cannot be traveled to, owned, earned, worn or consumed. Happiness is the spiritual experience of living every minute with love, grace and gratitude.

- Denis Waitley

The truest greatness lies in being kind, the truest wisdom in a happy mind.

- Ella Wheeler Wilcox

I can think of nothing less pleasurable than a life devoted to pleasure.

- John D. Rockfeller

The pursuit of happiness is a most ridiculous phrase, if you pursue happiness you'll never find it.

- C. P. Snow

The truth which has made us free will in the end make us glad also.

- Felix Adler

Happiness comes when your work and words are of benefit to yourself and others.

- Buddha

If only we'd stop trying to be happy we'd have a pretty good time.

- Edith Wharton

Let us be grateful to people who make us happy; they are the charming gardeners who make our souls blossom.

- Marcel Proust

The richness I achieve comes from Nature, the source of my inspiration.

- Claude Monet

Happiness is as a butterfly which, when pursued, is always beyond our grasp, but which if you will sit down quietly, may alight upon you.

- Nathaniel Hawthorne

The truth is that our finest moments are most likely to occur when we are feeling deeply uncomfortable, unhappy, or unfulfilled. For it is only in such moments, propelled by our discomfort, that we are likely to step out of our ruts and start searching for different ways or truer answers.

- M. Scott Peck

If you want others to be happy, practice compassion. If you want to be happy, practice compassion.

- Tenzin Gyatso, 14th Dalai Lama

Those who bring sunshine into the lives of others, cannot keep it from themselves.

- James M. Barrie

Happiness, it seems to me, consists of two things: first, in being where you belong, and second and best in comfortably going through everyday life, that is, having had a good night's sleep and not being hurt by new shoes.

- Theodor Fontane

Happiness often sneaks in through a door you didn't know you left open.

- John Barrymore

Growth itself contains the germ of happiness.

- Pearl S. Buck

What we call the secret of happiness is no more a secret than our willingness to choose life.

- Leo Buscaglia

There is no duty we so underrate as the duty of being happy. By being happy we sow anonymous benefits upon the world.

- Robert Louis Stevenson

We all live with the objective of being happy; our lives are all different and yet the same.

- Anne Frank

When one door of happiness closes, another opens; but often we look so long at the closed door that we do not see the one which has been opened for us.

- Helen Keller

The best remedy for those who are afraid, lonely or unhappy is to go outside, somewhere where they can be quiet, alone with the heavens, nature and God. Because only then does one feel that all is as it should be and that God wishes to see people happy, amidst the simple beauty of nature.

- Anne Frank

Success is not the key to happiness. Happiness is the key to success. If you love what you are doing, you will be successful.

- Albert Schweitzer

People spend a lifetime searching for happiness; looking for peace. They chase idle dreams, addictions, religions, even other people, hoping to fill the emptiness that plagues them. The irony is the only place they ever needed to search was within.

- Ramona L. Anderson

It's pretty hard to tell what does bring happiness. Poverty an' wealth have both failed.

- Kin Hubbard

Why not let people differ about their answers to the great mysteries of the Universe? Let each seek one's own way to the highest, to one's own sense of supreme loyalty in life, one's ideal of life. Let each philosophy, each worldview bring forth its truth and beauty to a larger perspective, that people may grow in vision, stature and dedication.

- Algernon Black

When we feel love and kindness toward others, it not only makes others feel loved and cared for, but it helps us also to develop inner happiness and peace.

- Tenzin Gyatso, 14th Dalai Lama

The ultimate end of education is happiness or a good human life, a life enriched by the possession of every kind of good, by the enjoyment of every type of satisfaction.

- Mortimer Adler

Happiness: We rarely feel it.
I would buy it, beg it, steal it,
Pay in coins of dripping blood
For this one transcendent good.

- Amy Lowell

There is a wonderful mythical law of nature that the three things we crave most in life happiness, freedom, and peace of mind are always attained by giving them to someone else.

- Peyton Conway March

Unhappiness is best defined as the difference between our talents and our expectations.

- Edward de B

The world has to learn that the actual pleasure derived from material things is of rather low quality on the whole and less even in quantity than it looks to those who have not tried it.

You can never get enough of what you don't need to make you happy.

— *Eric Hoffer*

I don't know what your destiny will be, but one thing I do know: the only ones among you who will be really happy are those who have sought and found how to serve.

— *Albert Schweitzer*

There are as many nights as days, and the one is just as long as the other in the year's course. Even a happy life cannot be without a measure of darkness, and the word 'happy' would lose its meaning if it were not balanced by sadness.

— *Carl Jung*

Sanity and happiness are an impossible combination.

— *Mark Twain*

Happiness is not in the mere possession of money; it lies in the joy of achievement, in the thrill of creative effort.

— *Franklin D. Roosevelt*

The most I can do for my friend is simply to be his friend. I have no wealth to bestow on him. If he knows that I am happy in loving him, he will want no other reward. Is not friendship divine in this?

— *Henry David Thoreau*

Happiness is when what you think, what you say, and what you do are in harmony.

— *Mohandas K. Gandhi*

Happiness is a Swedish sunset it is there for all, but

most of us look the other way and lose it.

— *Mark Twain*

But friendship is precious, not only in the shade, but in the sunshine of life; and thanks to a benevolent arrangement of things, the greater part of life is sunshine.

— *Thomas Jefferson*

Independence is happiness.

— *Susan B. Anthony*

Many people have a wrong idea of what constitutes true happiness. It is not attained through self-gratification, but through fidelity to a worthy purpose.

— *Helen Keller*

The perfection of wisdom, and the end of true philosophy is to proportion our wants to our possessions, our ambitions to our capacities, we will then be a happy and a virtuous people.

— *Mark Twain*

Happiness is having a large, loving, caring, close-knit family in another city.

— *George Burns*

The true way to render ourselves happy is to love our work and find in it our pleasure.

— *Francoise de Motteville*

The greatest part of our happiness depends on our dispositions, not our circumstances.

— *Martha Washington*

Happiness is not so much in having as sharing. We make a living by what we get, but we make a life by what we give.

— *Norman MacEwan*

When you have once seen the glow of happiness on the

face of a beloved person, you know that a man can have no vocation but to awaken that light on the faces surrounding him; and you are torn by the thought of the unhappiness and night you cast, by the mere fact of living, in the hearts you encounter.

- Albert Camus

You don't develop courage by being happy in your relationships everyday. You develop it by surviving difficult times and challenging adversity.

- Barbara De Angelis

Love is a condition in which the happiness of another person is essential to your own.

- Robert Heinlein

The mind is its own place, and in itself, can make heaven of Hell, and a hell of Heaven.

- John Milton

The happiness that is genuinely satisfying is accompanied by the fullest exercise of our faculties and the fullest realization of the world in which we live.

- Bertrand Russell

Wisdom is the supreme part of happiness.

- Sophocles

Sometimes your joy is the source of your smile, but sometimes your smile can be the source of your joy.

- Thich Nhat Hanh

That man is richest whose pleasures are cheapest.

- Henry David Thoreau

All seasons are beautiful for the person who carries happiness within.

- Horace Friess

To fill the hour that is happiness.

- Ralph Waldo Emerson

The Grand essentials of happiness are: something to do, something to love, and something to hope for.

- Allan K. Chalmers

It is only possible to live happily ever after on a day to day basis.

- Margaret Bonnano

Happiness belongs to the self-sufficient

- Aristotle

I don't know why we are here, but I'm pretty sure that it is not in order to enjoy ourselves.

- Ludwig Wittgenstein

Here we are the way politics ought to be in America; the politics of happiness, the politics of purpose and the politics of joy.

- Hubert H. Humphrey

Whoever is happy will make others happy, too.

- Mark Twain

Consider the following. We humans are social beings. We come into the world as the result of others' actions. We survive here in dependence on others. Whether we like it or not, there is hardly a moment of our lives when we do not benefit from others' activities. For this reason it is hardly surprising that most of our happiness arises in the context of our relationships with others.

- Tenzin Gyatso, 14th Dalai Lama

Remember happiness doesn't depend upon who you are or what you have; it depends solely on what you think.

-Dale Carnegie

The first recipe of **happiness** — avoid too lengthy meditations on the past.

— Andre Maurois

That is happiness — to be dissolved into something complete and great.

— Willa Cather

The more we express our **gratitude** to God for our blessings, the more he will bring to our mind other blessings. The more we are aware of to be grateful for, the happier we become.

— Ezra Taft Benson

If I feel depressed, I go to work. Work is always an antidote to depression.

— Eleanor Roosevelt

Happiness is the best medicine.

— Rowan Hooper

Life is a matter of passing the time enjoyably. There may be other things in life, but I've been too busy passing my time enjoyably to think very deeply about them.

— Peter Cook

Make one person happy each day and in forty years you will have made 14,600 human beings happy for a little time at least.

— Charles Wiley

When you finally allow yourself to trust joy and embrace it, you will find you dance with everything.

— Emanuel

Don't waste a minute being unhappy. If one window closes — run to the next window — or break down a door.

— Anonymous

True happiness arises in the first place from enjoyment of oneself.

-Joseph Addition

The aim of life is to live and to live means to be aware — joyously, drunkenly, serenely, divinely aware.

-Henry Miller

To be happy, do not add to your possessions, but subtract from your desires.

-Unknown

Live with your whole being all the days of your life. Your reward will be true happiness.

-Rebecca Thomas Shane

Cheerfulness keeps up a kind of daylight in the mind and fills it with a steady and perpetual serenity.

-Joseph Addison

To live long and achieve happiness, cultivate the art of radiating happiness.

-Malcolm Forbes

Looking forward to things is half the pleasure of them.

-Lucy Maud Montgomery

The real joy of life is in its play. Play is anything we do for the joy and love of doing it, apart from any profit, compulsion, or sense of duty. It is the real joy of living.

-Walter Rauschbusch

Perceive and rejoice that life is abundant, that beauty and goodness are amply available . . . that your happiness is in your hands.

-Paul Hodges

The moments of happiness we enjoy take us by surprise. It is not that we seize them, but they seize us.

-Ashley Montagu

Even if happiness forgets you a little bit, never completely forget about it.
— *James Prevert*

To pursue joy is to lose it. The only way to get it is to follow steadily the path of duty, without thinking of joy, and then, like sheep, it comes most surely, unsought.
— *A. Marc Lauren*

Happiness does not consist in things, but in the relish we have of them . . .
— *Francois duc de la Rochefoucald*

You don't have to know how to sing, it's feeling as though you want to that makes the day happy and successful.
— *Monica Crane*

What a wonderful life I've had. I only wish I had realized it sooner.
— *Collette*

Happiness is really a deep harmonious inner satisfaction and approval.
— *Francis Wilshire*

A certain simplicity of living is usually necessary to happiness.
— *Henry D. Chapin*

Always remember to forget the things that made you sad, but never forget to remember the things that made you glad.
— *Victor Borge*

Enjoy your life without comparing it to others.
— *Condobcet*

I am not fully dressed until I adorn myself with a smile. May you be truly blessed to always glitter with a radiance that shines from deep within you.

— *Barbara Becker Holstein*

I'm going to be happy today,
Though the skies may be cloudy and gray,
No matter what may come my way,
I'm going to be happy today.

— *Ella Wheeler Wilcox*

The true secret of happiness lies in taking a genuine interest in all the details of daily life and elevating them to an art.

— *William Morris*

His aspiration to the heights;
When he attains his goal, he cools
And longs for other distant flights.

— *Kahlil Gibran*

Happiness is a state of activity.

— *Aristotle*

Men spend their lives in anticipations, in determining to be vastly happy at some period when they have time. But the present time has one advantage over every other — it is our own. Past opportunities are gone, future have not come. We may lay in a stock of pleasures, as we would lay in a stock of wine; but if we defer the tasting of them too long, we shall find that both are soured by age.

— *Charles Caleb Colton*

If thou wilt make a man happy, add not unto his riches but take away from his desires.

— *Epicurus*

In seeking happiness for others, you find it for yourself.

— *Unknown*

The secret of happiness is not in doing what one likes, but in liking what one does.

- James M. Barrie

To be happy, we must not be too concerned with others.

- Albert Camus

If you want happiness for an hour — take a nap.

If you want happiness for a day — go fishing.

If you want happiness for a year — inherit a fortune.

If you want happiness for a lifetime — help someone else.

- Chinese Proverb

If men would consider not so much wherein they differ, as wherein they agree, there would be far less of uncharitableness and angry feeling in the world.

- Joseph Addison

Happiness comes of the capacity to feel deeply, to enjoy simply, to think freely, to risk life, to be needed.

-Storm Jameson

The Grand essentials of happiness are: something to do, something to love, and something to hope for.

-Allan K. Chalmers

The best remedy for those who are afraid, lonely or unhappy is to go outside, somewhere where they can be quiet, alone with the heavens, nature and God. Because only then does one feel that all is as it should be and that God wishes to see people happy, amidst the simple beauty of nature.

-Anne Frank

Action may not always bring happiness, but there is no happiness without action.

-Benjamin Disraeli

In the path of our happiness shall we find the learning for which we have chosen this lifetime.

-Richard Bach

It is neither wealth nor splendor; but tranquility and occupation which give happiness.

-Thomas Jefferson

Happiness comes when your work and words are of benefit to yourself and others.

-Buddha

Keep your face to the sunshine and you cannot see the shadows.

- Helen Keller

You can never get enough of what you don't need to make you happy.

- Eric Hoffer

We have no more right to consume happiness without producing it than to consume wealth without producing it.

- George Bernard Shaw

The greatest happiness you can have is knowing that you do not necessarily require happiness.

- William Saroyan

Happiness is a function of accepting what is.

- Werner Erhard

The essentials to happiness are something to love, something to do, and something to hope for.

- William Blake

Most people are about as happy as they make up their minds to be.

- Abraham Lincoln

Happiness is like a kiss. You must share it to enjoy it.

- Bernard Melzer

Happiness is not something you postpone for the future; it is something you design for the present.

- Jim Rohn

Happiness is the meaning and the purpose of life, the whole aim and end of human existence.

- Aristotle

Happiness, that grand mistress of the ceremonies in the dance of life, impels us through all its mazes and meanderings, but leads none of us by the same route.

-Charles Caleb Colton

The highest happiness of man is to have probed what is knowable and quietly to revere what is unknowable.

-Johann Wolfgang von Goethe

Family life is the source of the greatest human happiness. This happiness is the simplest and least costly kind, and it cannot be purchased with money. But it can be increased if we do two things: if we recognize and uphold the essential values of family life and if we get and keep control of the process of social change so as to make it give us what is needed to make family life perform its essential functions.

-Robert J. Havighurst

Action may not always bring happiness; but there is no happiness without action.

-Benjamin Disraeli

It makes no difference where you go, there you are. And it makes no difference what you have, there's always more to want. Until you are happy with who you are, you will never be happy because of what you have.

-Zig Ziglar

To see a world in a grain of sand and heaven in a wild flower,

Hold infinity in the palm of your hand and eternity in an hour.

- William Blake

The most perfect society is that whose purpose is the universal and supreme happiness.

- Gottfried Wilhelm Leibniz

A string of excited, fugitive, miscellaneous pleasures is not happiness; happiness resides in imaginative reflection and judgment, when the picture of one's life, or of human life, as it truly has been or is, satisfies the will, and is gladly accepted.

- George Santayana

Happiness always looks small while you hold it in your hands, but let it go, and you learn at once how big and precious it is.

- Maxim Gorky

Happiness is like a sunbeam, which the least shadow intercepts.

- Chinese proverb

Drugs bring us to the gates of paradise, then keep us from entering.

- Mason Cooley

The happiest people seem to be those who have no particular cause for being happy except that they are so.

- William Ralph Inge

The happy man's without a shirt.

- John Heywood

Men can only be happy when they do not assume that the object of life is happiness.

- George Orwell

The secret of happiness is to face the world is horrible, horrible, horrible.

- Bertrand Russell

It is better to be happy for a moment and be burned up with beauty than to live a long time and be bored all the while.

- Don Marquis

The mind is its own place, and in itself, can make a Heaven of Hell, a Hell of Heaven.

- John Milton

It is not God's will merely that we should be happy, but that we should make ourselves happy.

- Immanuel Kant

He who lives happiest has forgotten most.

- Robert Anton Wilson

The happy think a lifetime short, but to the unhappy one night can be an eternity.

- Lucian

To describe happiness is to diminish it.

- Henri B. Stendhal

Hope is itself a species of happiness, and, perhaps, the chief happiness which this world affords.

- Samuel Johnson

The surest way to happiness is to lose yourself in a cause greater than yourself.

- Unknown

Remember, happiness doesn't depend upon who you are or what you have, it depends solely upon what you think.

- Dale Carnegie

Happiness is unrepentant pleasure.

- Socrates

Happiness is a very pretty thing to feel, but very dry to talk about.

- Jeremy Bentham

The essence of philosophy is that a man should so live that his happiness shall depend as little as possible on external things.

- Epictetus

Pleasure is the only thing to live for. Nothing ages like happiness.

- Oscar Wilde

Most of us believe in trying to make other people happy only if they can be happy in ways which we approve.

- Robert S. Lynd

Happiness in intelligent people is the rarest thing I know.

- Ernest Hemingway

Happiness is the meaning and the purpose of life, the whole aim and end of human existence.

- Aristotle

Happiness is like those palaces in fairy tales whose gates are guarded by dragons: we must fight in order to conquer it.

- Alexandre Dumas

To be happy is not the purpose of our being rather it is to deserve happiness.

- Johann G. Fichte

Act in such a way that you will be worthy of being happy.

- Immanuel Kant

The happier the moment the shorter.

— *Pliny The Elder*

Happiness is the only good. The time to be happy is now. The place to be happy is here. The way to be happy is to make others so.

— *Robert Green Ingersoll*

If you want to understand the meaning of happiness, you must see it as a reward and not as a goal.

— *Antoine de Saint-Exupery*

Happiness does not lie in happiness, but in the achievement of it.

— *Fyodor Dostoevsky*

A world full of happiness is not beyond human power to create; the obstacles imposed by inanimate nature are not insuperable. The real obstacles lie in the heart of man, and the cure for these is a firm hope, informed and fortified by thought.

— *Bertrand Russell*

Happiness depends, as Nature shows, less on exterior things than most suppose.

— *William Cowper*

Before we set our hearts too much upon anything, let us examine how happy they are, who already possess it.

— *François Duc de La Rochefoucauld*

Happiness in intelligent people is the rarest thing I know.

— *Ernest Hemingway*

I am happy and content because I think I am.

— *Alain-Rene Lesage*

Happiness, though an indefinite concept, is the goal of all rational beings.

- Immanuel Kant

The greatest happiness of the greatest number is the foundation of morals and legislation.

- Jeremy Bentham

It appeared to me obvious that the happiness of mankind should be the aim of all action, and I discovered to my surprise that there were those who thought otherwise.

- Bertrand Russell

Let no man be called happy before his death. Till then, he is not happy, only lucky.

- Solon

To be happy is to be able to become aware of oneself without fright.

- Walter Benjamin

Scarcely one person in a thousand is capable of tasting the happiness of others.

- Henry Fielding

There is nothing which has yet been contrived by man, by which so much happiness is produced as by a good tavern or inn.

- Samuel Johnson

Happiness consumes itself like a flame. It cannot burn for ever, it must go out, and the presentiment of its end destroys it at its very peak.

- J. August Strindberg

The important question is not, what will yield to man a few scattered pleasures, but what will render his life happy on the whole amount.

- Joseph Addison

Happiness is like manna; it is to be gathered in grains, and enjoyed every day. It will not keep; it cannot be accumulated; nor have we got to go out of ourselves or into remote places to gather it, since it has rained down from a Heaven, at our very door.

- Tryon Edwards

Happiness is the highest good, being a realization and perfect practice of virtue, which some can attain, while others have little or none of it.

- Aristotle

Happiness serves hardly any other purpose than to make unhappiness possible.

- Marcel Proust

If you observe a really happy man you will find him building a boat, writing a symphony, educating his son, growing double dahlias in his garden, or looking for dinosaur eggs in the Gobi desert. He will not be searching for happiness as if it were a collar button that has rolled under the radiator. He will not be striving for it as a goal in itself. He will have become aware that he is happy in the course of living life twenty-four crowded hours of the day.

W. Beran Wolfe

Happiness is in the taste, and not in the things.

- La Rochefoucauld

The happiness which we receive from ourselves is greater than that which we obtain from our surroundings. The world in which a person lives shapes itself chiefly by the way in which he or she looks at it.

- Arthur Schopenhauer

Happiness resides not in possessions, and not in gold, happiness dwells in the soul.

- Democritus

If there were in the world today any large number of people who desired their own happiness more than they desired the unhappiness of others, we could have paradise in a few years.

- Bertrand Russell

There is no happiness; there are only moments of happiness.

- Spanish Proverb

Happiness ain't a thing in itself — it's only a contrast with something that ain't pleasant.

- Mark Twain

The most exciting happiness is the happiness generated by forces beyond your control.

- Ogden Nash

All men seek happiness. This is without exception. Whatever different means they employ, they all tend to this end. The cause of some going to war, and of others avoiding it, is the same desire in both, attended with different views. This is the motive of every action of every man, even of those who hang themselves.

- Blaise Pascal

Life's greatest happiness is to be convinced we are loved.

- Victor Hugo

Do not speak of your happiness to one less fortunate than yourself.

- Plutarch

When a man has lost all happiness, he's not alive. Call him a breathing corpse.

- Sophocles

Indeed, man wishes to be happy even when he so lives as to make happiness impossible.

- St. Augustine

The two enemies of human happiness are pain and boredom.

- Arthur Schopenhauer

Let us be grateful to people who make us happy; they are the charming gardeners who make our souls blossom.

- Marcel Proust

Really high-minded people are indifferent to happiness, especially other people's.

- Bertrand Russell

The great end of all human industry is the attainment of happiness. For this were arts invented, sciences cultivated, laws ordained, and societies modeled, by the most profound wisdom of patriots and legislators. Even the lonely savage, who lies exposed to the inclemency of the elements and the fury of wild beasts, forgets not, for a moment, this grand object of his being.

- David Hume

Happiness is an imaginary condition, formerly often attributed by the living to the dead, now usually attributed by adults to children, and by children to adults.

- Thomas Szasz

He is happy that knoweth not himself to be otherwise.

- Thomas Fuller

He who binds to himself a joy
Does the winged life destroy;
But he who kisses the joy as it flies
Lives in eternity's sun rise.

- William Blake

I have learned to seek my happiness by limiting my desires, rather than in attempting to satisfy them.

- John Stuart Mill

Be happy. It's one way of being wise.

- Colette

Those who seek happiness miss it, and those who discuss it, lack it.

- Holbrook Jackson

It is not God's will merely that we should be happy, but that we should make ourselves happy.

- Immanuel Kant

The highest happiness of man ... is to have probed what is knowable and quietly to revere what is unknowable.

- Goethe

Happiness is the only sanction of life; where happiness fails, existence becomes a mad lamentable experiment.

- George Santayana

The more refined one is, the more unhappy.

- Anton Chekhov

How to gain, how to keep, and how to recover happiness is in fact for most men at all times the secret motive for all they do.

- William James

Happiness is an attitude. We either make ourselves miserable, or happy and strong. The amount of work is the same.

- Francesca Reigler

Science suggests that when you smile, whether you feel happy or not, your mood will be elevated. So smile all the time! In addition having enough money to pay the bills allows you to focus your energies on more productive

aspects of your life, such a the pursuit of happiness as opposed to keeping the 'wolves from the door'.
— *Unknown*

When you confront a problem you begin to solve it.
— *Rudy Guiliani*

Happiness depends upon ourselves.
— *Aristotle*

Life's challenges are not supposed to paralyze you, they're supposed to help you discover who you are.
— *Bernice Johnson Reagon*

Don't think of problems as difficulties. Think of them as opportunities for action.
— *Unknown*

Most of the important things in the world have been accomplished by people who have kept on trying when there seemed to be no hope at all.
— *Dale Carnegie*

Real happiness comes from inside. Nobody can give it to you.
— *Sharon Stone*

Believe it is possible to solve your problem. Tremendous things happen to the believer. So believe the answer will come. It will.
— *Norman Vincent Peale*

To be successful you must accept all challenges that come your way. You can't just accept the ones you like.
— *Mike Gafka*

The happiness of your life depends on the quality of your thoughts.
— *Marcus A. Antoninus*

In order to be happy you need a good dog, a good woman, and ready money.

- Benjamin Franklin

If you can't be happy where you are, it's a cinch you can't be happy where you ain't.

- Charles "Tremendous" Jones

If you were happy every day of your life you wouldn't be a human being, you'd be a game show host.

- Gabriel Heatter

Success is getting what you want. Happiness is liking what you get.

- H. Jackson Brown

If you ever find happiness by hunting for it, you will find it as the old woman did her lost spectacles. Safe on her own nose all the time.

- Josh Billings

If you want to be happy, be.

- Leo Tolstoy

Man is fond of counting his troubles, but he does not count his joys. If he counted them up as he ought to, he would see that every lot has enough happiness provided for it.

- Fyodor Dostoevsky

We tend to forget that happiness doesn't come as a result of getting something we don't have, but rather of recognizing and appreciating what we do have.

- Frederick Keonig

Happiness comes from spiritual wealth, not material wealth... Happiness comes from giving, not getting. If we try hard to bring happiness to others, we cannot stop it from coming to us also. To get joy, we must give it, and to keep joy, we must scatter it.

— *John Templeton*

The Grand essentials of happiness are: something to do, something to love, and something to hope for.

— *Allan K. Chalmers*

People take different roads seeking fulfillment and happiness. Just because they're not on your road doesn't mean they've gotten lost.

— *H. Jackson Brown, Jr.*

We are long before we are convinced that happiness is never to be found, and each believes it possessed by others, to keep alive the hope of obtaining it for himself.

— *Samuel Johnson*

He is happiest, be he king or peasant, who finds peace in his home.

— *Johann von Goethe*

I have no money, no resources, no hopes. I am the happiest man alive.

— *Henry Miller*

Don't worry, be happy.

— *Bobby McFerrin*

Happiness is the meaning and the purpose of life, the whole aim and end of human existence.

— *Aristotle*

Be happy. It's one way of being wise.

— *Sidonie Gabrielle*

We tend to forget that happiness doesn't come as a result of getting something we don't have, but rather of recognizing and appreciating what we do have.

— *Frederick Keonig*

Some people walk in the rain. Others just get wet.

- Roger Miller

The reason people find it so hard to be happy is that they always see the past better than it was, the present worse than it is, and the future less resolved than it will be.

- Marcel Pagnol

Success is not the key to happiness.

Happiness is the key to success.

If you love what you are doing, you will be successful.

- Albert Schweitzer

You will never be happy if you continue to search for what happiness consists of.

You will never live if you are looking for the meaning of life.

- Albert Camus

People love others not for who they are but for how they make them feel.

- Irwin Federman

Some cause happiness wherever they go; others whenever they go.

- Oscar Wilde

The most wasted of all days is one without laughter.

- E.E. Cummings

Singing to my dogs every morning.

- Andrew S.

Watching the sun creep out of the water as it rises into a new day.

- Julia W.

Watching a kid with the giggles and then getting them yourself.

- Jamie H.

Listening to a gentle rain falling on a metal roof.

- Jana B.

Knowing that it takes just a few kind words and a smile to make someone feel loved and needed.

- Jennifer R.

Catching spring fever and not being sick with it. Just enjoying it!

- Lisa R.

That feeling you get after you have selflessly helped someone who needed it.

- Mary G.

Happiness is coming home after a hard day at work to find your selfless animals waiting at the door so excited to see you!

- Corey B.

Knowing that each day you wake up is another day God has given you to live, laugh and love with all your heart. Acceptance of who "you" are!!!

- Kim H.

The ability to create, connect and live my life outside the boxes that people find themselves in now.

- Hunter A.

Enjoying what you have.

- Tracy M.

Hearing my son laugh.

Mariana El.

Finding your lost dog on the porch the next morning.

- Casey S.

Making someone happy.

- Forrest M.

Knowing exactly what you want out of life, and not being afraid to go after it. Life is too short for wasted dreams!

- Stephanie E.

Watching your children grow.

- Wayne L.

Being alone in your car driving with no distractions, no radio and remembering something or someone that made you smile then and makes you smile in that moment...the good stuff...the good thought...the happy thought...the radiant thought that makes you smile from the inside out.

- Rowena W.

Laughing first thing every morning.

- Larry J.

Is building something that lasts.

- Oscar S.

Not comparing yourself to others.

- Henry K.

Life outside the Culture of Busy.

- Andy H.

Having three dogs.

- Faron W.

Hand-holding walks with my husband.

- Francis W.

A sitting together for family dinner.

Joey P.

A place to call home.

- Burk L.

Taking time to appreciate the little things.

- Terry H.

Saying "I love you" and hearing it back.

- Bella H.

A contagious smile.

- Russell R.

Remembering that life is short and that each moment counts.

- Lisa M.

Most folks are about as happy as they make up their minds to be.

- Abraham Lincoln

Happiness is an inside job.

- William Arthur Ward

Happiness is being married to your best friend.

- Barbara Weeks

The secret of happiness is to make others believe they are the cause of it.

- Al Batt

Happiness is often the result of being too busy to be miserable.

- Anonymous

Happiness is nothing more than good health and a bad memory.

- Albert Schweitzer

Happiness isn't a static thing; it's the quest for happiness that allows us to think we're happy, while we continue to search for more.

- Greg Webster

The happiness of a man in this life does not consist in the absence but in the mastery of his passions.

- Alfred Lord Tennyson

The discovery of a new dish does more for human happiness than the discovery of a new star.

- Anthelme Brillat

Happiness is that state of consciousness which proceeds from the achievement of one's values.

- Ayn Rand

A person is never happy except at the price of some ignorance.

- Anatole France

The pursuit of happiness is a most ridiculous phrase; if you pursue happiness you'll never find it.

- C. P. Snow

Sometimes it's hard to avoid the happiness of others.

- David Assael

Man is the artificer of his own happiness.

- Henry David Thoreau

If we cannot live so as to be happy, let us least live so as to deserve it.

- Immanuel Hermann Fichte

Thus happiness depends, as Nature shows, less on exterior things than most suppose.

- William Cowper

The foolish man seeks happiness in the distance, the wise grows it under his feet.

- James Oppenheim

True happiness is of a retired nature, and an enemy to pomp and noise; it arises, in the first place, from the enjoyment of one's self, and in the next from the friendship and conversation of a few select companions.

- Joseph Addison

Laughing is the sensation of feeling good all over and showing it principally in one spot.

- Josh Billings

Hold him alone truly fortunate who has ended his life in happy well-being.

- Aeschylus

Happiness: a good bank account, a good cook and a good digestion.

- Jean Jacques Rousseau

Real happiness is cheap enough, yet how dearly we pay for its counterfeit.

- Hosea Ballou

All who joy would win Must share it. Happiness was born a twin.

- Lord Byron (George Gordon Noel Byron)

Happiness is a choice that requires effort at times.

- Aeschylus

Cherish all your happy moments: they make a fine cushion for old age.

- Christopher Morley

Slow down and enjoy life. It's not only the scenery you miss by going too fast—you also miss the sense of where you are going and why.

- Eddie Cantor

To be stupid, selfish, and have good health are three requirements for happiness, though if stupidity is lacking, all is lost.

- Gustave Flaubert

Many persons have a wrong idea of what constitutes true happiness. It is not attained through self-gratification but through fidelity to a worthy purpose.

- Helen Keller

A lifetime of happiness! No man alive could bear it. It would be hell on earth.

- George Bernard Shaw

This is the best kind of voyeurism, hearing joy from your neighbors.

- Chuck Sigars

Happiness is good health and a bad memory.

- Cesare di Bonesana Beccaria

Happiness is the art of never holding in your mind the memory of any unpleasant thing that has passed.

- Anonymous

People take different roads seeking fulfillment and happiness. Just because they're not on your road doesn't mean they've gotten lost.

- Cesare di Bonesana Beccaria

Happiness is having a large, loving, caring, close-knit family in another city.

- George Burns

But what is happiness except the simple harmony between a man and the life he leads?

- Lord Byron (George Gordon Noel Byron)

Oh, Mirth and Innocence! Oh, Milk and Water! Ye happy mixture of more happy days!

- Lord Byron (George Gordon Noel Byron)

Happiness depends upon ourselves.

- Aristotle

We think a happy life consists in tranquility of mind.

- Tullius Cicero)

Happiness seems made to be shared.

- Pierre Corneille

If solid happiness we prize, Within our breast this jewel lies, And they are fools who roam; The world has nothing to bestow, From our own selves our bliss must flow, And that dear hut, our home.

— *Nathaniel Cotton*

There comes For ever something between us and what We deem our happiness.

— *Lord Byron (George Gordon Noel Byron)*

Domestic Happiness, thou only bliss of Paradise that hast survived the Fall!

— *William Cowper*

Happiness lies in our own backyard, but it's probably well hidden by crabgrass.

— *Anonymous*

Who is the happiest of men? He who values the merits of others, And in their pleasure takes joy, even as though t'were his own.

— *Johann Wolfgang von Goethe*

Happiness comes through doors you didn't even know you left open.

— *Anonymous*

Happiness is not best achieved by those who seek it directly.

— *Bertrand Russell*

Happiness is different from pleasure. Happiness has something to do with struggling and enduring and accomplishing.

— *George Sheehan*

Happiness is not in our circumstance but in ourselves. It is not something we see, like a rainbow, or feel, like the heat of a fire. Happiness is something we are.

- John B. Sheerin

Happiness is essentially a state of going somewhere, wholeheartedly, one-directionally, without regret or reservation.

- William H. Sheldon

Happiness is a wine of the rarest vintage, and seems insipid to a vulgar taste.

- Logan Pearsall Smith

Happiness has many roots, but none more important than security.

- E. R. Stettinius, Jr.

Happiness consists in activity; such as the constitution of our nature; it is a running stream, and not a stagnant pool.

- Anonymous

The highest happiness, the purest joys of life, wear out at last.

- Johann Wolfgang von Goethe

Happiness is like a butterfly. The more you chase it, the more it eludes you. But if you turn your attention to other things, It comes and sits softly on your shoulder.

- Anonymous

Happiness is an attitude of mind, born of the simple determination to be happy under all outward circumstances.

- J. Donald Walters

Money can't buy you happiness, but it does bring you a more pleasant form of misery.

- Milligan

Happiness is when what you think, what you say, and

what you do are in harmony. Apparently Gandhi didn't buy the "good fortune" or "prosperity" definitions. There's a reason they're considered obsolete definitions.

- Mahatma Gandhi

Remember happiness doesn't depend upon who you are or what you have; it depends solely on what you think.

- Dale Carnegie

True happiness is not attained through self-gratification, but through fidelity to a worthy purpose.

- Helen Keller

You will never be happier than you expect. To change your happiness, change your expectation.

- Bette Davis

Happiness is a butterfly, which, when pursued, is always just beyond your grasp, but which, if you sit down quietly, may alight upon you.

- Nathaniel Hawthorne

Happiness is the only good. The time to be happy is now. The place to be happy is here. The way to be happy is to make others so.

- Robert G. Ingersoll

To the man who pleases him, God gives wisdom, knowledge and happiness.

- Solomon

Happiness can be defined, in part at least, as the fruit of the desire and ability to sacrifice what we want now for what we want eventually.

- Stephen Covey

Realize that true happiness lies within you. Waste no time and effort searching for peace and contentment and joy in the world outside. Remember that there is no happiness in having or in getting, but only in giving. Reach out. Share. Smile. Hug. Happiness is a perfume you cannot pour on others without getting a few drops on yourself.

- Og Mandino

Happiness: a good bank account, a good cook, and a good digestion.

- Jean-Jacques Rousseau

Happiness ain't a thing in itself, it's only a contrast with something that ain't pleasant.

- Mark Twain

By all means marry: If you get a good wife, you'll become happy; if you get a bad one, you'll become a philosopher.

- Socrates

50. Reward Yourself and Be Happy

The other day my wife, Sushila was sharing with me an important idea of happiness. It so happened that after an usual morning walk I told Sushila that I am now having a busy day writing a book for happiness and that I want that the book should contain only the practical aspects relating to happiness. I continued saying that I am only interested to tell my readers something great, something innovative, something practical about happiness.

I continued asking Sushila to explain me at least one way of deriving her own derive happiness. Sushila now told her own thinking and own formula of deriving happiness in a practical manner. She continued saying that rewarding yourself is one single golden mantra in which she has great faith for her happiness.

After listening to her I told her that I could not get even ABCD about what she has to say. She now explained her view point and her philosophy on happiness.

Sushila said that I have my own style of being happy and with that style whenever she does some work or some activity which provides her a sense of contentment, a sense of fulfillment or a sense of doing something for someone, then she would like to get herself rewarded.

The million dollar question now is who is to be rewarded? With twinkling eyes Sushila immediately said that she would like to reward herself for doing some important work or some main activity.

She continued further that if I do some work which I wanted to do it for a long time and when such work is complete, then I would like to give the reward of pizza to myself and immediately she would place her mobile phone by her lap, she would now telephone the Pizza Company and order for one Pizza to be sent out instantly. Similarly, Sushila would order an ice cream at the Ice Cream Parlour as soon as she would get fulfillment for doing some activity which she wanted to do.

Well, this is one another unique and special style of being happy. The morale of this actual life incident is that take resolution of rewarding yourself by some gift in that form which provides you happiness.

The theme of rewarding oneself brings happiness more closer to your heart. Now, I came to know of this unique happiness formula which in real life is being practised by my wife.

In common parlance of life we find that in most families the husbands are engrossed in the day to day office activities be it in service or be it in their own personal business and the time available for the family is very minimal. In such situation, the house wife gets bored and does not find a place of happiness in her day to day life.

Hence, such ladies in particular if they plan to reward themselves in the above manner for some work or activity done by them, then surely they will be enjoying happiness. If you have faith in this concept, then adopt right from today the concept of rewarding yourself to be happy.

The reward can be in the form of buying some good eatables for you or doing some special shopping for you and this reward comes to you by yourself mainly because you have completed certain activity which you have been waiting to do for a long time.

Getting rewarded yourself is a fun, a fun for happiness, so now go and enjoy your happiness with your own reward. What an innovative idea indeed.

51. Mediate on a Quotation and Be Happy

Just one line of wonderful message written by someone whom you have never met can be instrumental in providing your happiness. The fact remains that if you just read couple of lines from some book or you glance through couple of lines of some famous personality in the form of a quote, then suddenly you find that your mind has realised a deeper taste to that quote, then the chances are that you may be able to find your happiness by reading and going through the said quote again and again and again. Hence, once in a while from your busy schedule try to find out some quotation and spend half an hour to go into the depth of that quotation and once you are engrossed emotionally with that quotation, then surely you will find happiness derived by you just by that quotation. In spiritual language this activity can be known as Shakti Path. The Shakti or the power of the person who wrote particular lines of the quotation have been instrumental in encouraging your body and mind to absorb the thought of quotation and now as and when you read and read the said quotation your happiness increases.

I have read one quotation from Helen Keller which said "The best and most beautiful things in the world cannot be seen or even touched — they must be felt with the heart." When I read this quotation, I got inspired and I am also inspired that if the theme of this quotation is applied to happiness, then also this quote fits in the concept of providing better happiness to one and all. It is true that the happiness cannot be seen and cannot be touched and it has to be only felt within the heart. I feel that the readers of this book will be able to feel happiness in their heart if they follow what all has been written in this book. Hence, this quotation of Helen Keller really is very inspiring. It is emotional. It creates magic for everyone specially if you are going to believe in this simple two line quote. Similar would also be the situation with reference to love. Applying the above quote in the context of love, we come to the conclusion that even if love cannot be seen or even touched. It has to felt within the heart. Hence, this quotation appears personally to me to be very apt and you would also find dear to your heart but only if you become emotionally attached to this quotation.

My father R.N. Lakhotia edits a monthly magazine known as Excellent Living. This he has been doing so for last 25 years. Every month copies of this small little magazine are sent free of cost to thousands of persons in different parts of India. In this magazine the regular issue contains one page which is exclusive devoted to inspiring quotations. Last week when I was going through one of the old issues of the magazine, I found an interesting quote by Logan P. Smith which said that "There are two things to aim at in life, first to get what you want and after that to enjoy it. Only wisest of mankind achieve the second." A first reading of this quotation did not inspire me and I could not see anything very special but by chance this page of the magazine came to my table two-three times in a week and every time my focus would go on to this quotation. Now, I read the quotation, I felt my emotion and my meditation went deep into the contents of this quotation, I could feel a great big idea to provide happiness to me through this quotation. I was thinking that this quotation will really bring home for me something great, something unique to provide a sort of special happiness formula for me. Now, when I read this quotation after screening it bit by bit, I found a great big lesson of life, the lesson which inspires me, the lesson which makes me think about the mission and aim of life, the mission which directs me to derive happiness after one has achieved what one wants. I am now a great fan of this quotation. I am sure together with me thousands of my readers would be fan of this great big quotation which I feel is certainly going to provide incentive to you for better happiness in your life. If you want to be happy, then read this quotation again and again and finally implement the real classic hidden treasure of this quotation in your practical life by analysing your facts and your circumstances and then applying the theme and spirit of this quotation to your own practical life and then you find great happiness is at your door.

Now, firstly I want you to believe in the concept of deriving happiness by meditating on a "quotation." Believe in this fact that even in the past the world has been moved by the writings of some great men. In India also it is Swami Vivekananda whose writings have influenced the ages in the spiritual path. In the same manner I want first of all that you should have faith on this concept of deriving happiness by meditating on a quotation. Once you have the faith on this concept, then you find happiness at your door step whenever you find a great quotation. Now, applying this concept to the above mentioned quote of Logan P. Smith, we find that if we analyse the contents of this quotation, then we find that the contents of this quotation are apt for every person. It is apt for a person who is not so very rich. Equally it is apt for a person who is very rich and likewise another person who is filthy rich, even for him, this quotation would give him a thought to ponder, a thought to be happy about. For example, if we screen this quotation, we find that we should all do introspection at some point of time in our life whereby we aim to get what we want and once after putting in hard work of time, talent and treasure for a decade or more, we find that we have been able to achieve what we wanted in life. Now, then comes the time to enjoy what you have achieved. For example, you were born in a very ordinary family or in a poor family and you wanted to be rich. You wanted to make money. With the hard work and with the grace of the God you have now made money. So now you have been able to achieve the first aim in your life which was to make money. And now comes the time that you should enjoy the taste of this money. The meaning of this theme is that once you achieve a particular level of making money in your life, then now comes the occasion to devote your time and energy to test the enjoyment which can be derived by your money. Thus, can further be analysed by taking advantage of enjoying the life by visiting major foreign destinations to explore the world.

One can even enjoy through money the happiness which can be derived by contributing to the community we live in. Finally, in the end you will come to the conclusion that if you have been able to enjoy your money power, then surely it will provide happiness to you. Hence, concentrate right now on different quotes coming from different people in life.

I remember a small one line quote by Rita Mat Brown which says that one of the keys to happiness is bad memory. If you think this quotation from a long term perspective, then you will find that get lost with reference to the old bad memories of yours and then you find happiness coming closer to you. Likewise, another small line of Brain Tracy says that look for the good in every person and every situation. You will almost always find that the contents of this quotation are true. This again can be your happiness formula if you meditate on this quote. Thus, quotation can help you to face any adverse situation and can help you be positive in your life and you start realising that yes you can definitely find something good in every person, in every walk of life and in every situation.

This positive hope can be derived by you just by going through small or big quote by someone which if you read and read again, can be instrumental to provide happiness to you. I also recollect yet another quote from Charron Bierre which says that he who receives a benefit should never forget it, he who bestows should never remember it. Well, this one line again can be a source of happiness for you whether you are on the giver side or on the receiver side. For better results of this one line quote think of this quote again and again and apply the reality of this quote into your life. Similarly, Roger Bed Bussy once said that when we cannot have what we love, we must love what we have. This is really yet another happiness formula which will inspire every person in this world to be happy in all such situations and it gives emotional support of facing the world. I also was impressed the other day when I read a one line quote by H. Jackson Brown, Jr. which says that opportunities could also come to life. I repeated this quotation amongst my friends circle and soon I found that many persons got intoxicated with this single quotation and they got happiness because they could think and they could believe that yes opportunities could also come to their life also. Another one line by Charles Sumner has been instrumental in providing happiness to yet another friend of mine who is engaged with a voluntary social organisation. Here is the inspirational line by Charles: "No permanent failure can be found if accepted in labour which promotes the happiness of mankind." By reading this quotation again and again, this group of voluntary social people started rendering more efficient service to the humanity because in that service, they could see their happiness hidden behind it.

My dear friends, do develop the habit of reading quotations by top people. The more you read such quotation you come across more situations which would go to provide you an everlasting happiness for you and your family. All that you have to do is to analyse in depth meaning of the quotation and implement the contents of the subject matter of the quotation to your life cycle.

In this book, some good quotations are printed which will inspire you, yes they would surely do so.

52. New Medical Research for Your Health

Throughout the world various organisations are engaged in carrying out medical research in various fields. Summary of some of the recent findings as printed in recent newspapers are printed below which will bring surely some ray of hope for all those who suffer from these ailments:

Genes Linked to Heart Disease:

Thirteen new gene variants have been found to have connections with a high risk of developing heart disease in a large scale international study. The study, published Sunday in Nature Genetics, was one of the most far reaching in the past years. Led by researchers at the University of Leicester in the United Kingdom and University of Lubeck in Germany, it also involved 150 scientists from across Europe, Canada and the United States.

For this study, the international research group examined the complete genetic profiles of more than 22,000 people of European descent with coronary heart disease or a heart attack history. Then they compared the data to that of around 60,000 healthy people to validate the findings. The result show that of the total of 23 variants now know, seven are linked with levels of 'bad' and one is linked with high blood pressure, both of which are known risk factors for heart disease. But the others are not relevant to know about cardiovascular risk factors. Researchers said that the findings would provide clues to the new opportunities for future discovery and lead to more effective treatment plans.

The statistics of the World Health Organisation show that cardiovascular diseases claim 17.1 million lives every year; they are the world's biggest killers. The cost on medical devices and drugs for heart disease treatment amounts to billions of US Dollars every year.

New Research for Obese Adolescents

"Bariatric surgery" refers to several different surgical procedures designed to assist weight loss by limiting the amount of food someone eats or the amount they absorb during digestion. It has been used for several years to treat obesity in adults a new study published in the Journal Clinical Obesity reveals that bariatric surgery can result in significant weight loss in severely obese adolescents.

Led by Ange Alkenhead of the International Association for the Study of Obesity in London, England, researchers searched various databases for articles examining subjects less that 19 years of age reporting at least one year of postoperative follow-up.

The existing evidence suggests that bariatric surgery in older children results in significant weight loss and improvements in the quality of life. Establishing effective methods for treating severe obesity in children will not only reduce the prevalence of childhood obesity and related ill health, but inhibit the progression of obese children to obese adults, a crucial step in combating the epidemic.

Special Care for Denture Wearers

From its involvement in a healthy immune system to its role in cell growth, zinc is an essential mineral for the human body. Zinc deficiency is a worldwide problem that affects approximately 4 million people in the U.S. alone. Consumed naturally in the human diet, zinc can be found in food surces, such as beef, yogurt, eggs, and fish. Furthermore, zinc is widely used in dental products, specifically denture adhesives.

However, as with my herb, vitamin, or mineral, excess intake of zinc could pose a potential health hazard. Denture wearers are advised to pay special attention to the amount of zinc they consume, according to an article published in the March/April 2011 issue of General Dentistry, the peer-reviewed clinical journal of the Academy of General Dentistry (AGD0).

Brain Rhythm for Sleep Stability

A new study finds that a brain rhythm considered the hallmark of wakefulness not only persists inconspicuously during sleep but also signifies an individual's vulnerability to disturbance by the outside world. In their report in the March 3 PLOS one, the team from the Massachusetts General Hospital (MGH) Division of Sleep Medicine uses computerised EEG signal processing to detect subtle fluctuations in the alpha rhythm during sleep and shows that greater alpha intensity is associated with increased sleep fragility. The findings could lead to more precise approaches to inducing and supporting sleep.

Better Sleep for Employed and Self-Employed

As per Science Daily the employed and self-employed enjoy much better sleep than those out of work, according to Understanding Society, the world's largest longitudinal household study. Those who are unemployed are over 40% more likely to report difficulty staying asleep than those in employment (having controlled for age and gender differences). However, job satisfaction affects the quality of sleep with 33% of the most dissatisfied employees report poor sleep quality compared to only 18 percent of the most satisfied.

Analysis of the early data from Understanding Society based on 14,000 UK house holds found that over all the best sleep was reported by people with higher levels of education and married people. The type of work a person does also impacts on sleep, with those in routine occupations reporting worse sleep than those in professional occupations.

Professor Sara Arber at the University of Surrey who analysed the findings said : "Given the links between sleep, social and economic circumstances and poor health found in this and other surveys, health promotion campaigns should be open to the possibility that the increased incidence of sleep problems among the disadvantaged in society may be one factor leading to their poorer health."

Sleep Related New Medical Research

Here is a research report of the Understanding Society on. This organisation is funded by the Economic & Social Research Council. Here are their latest research report :-

- Women are more likely to report problem getting to sleep within 30 minutes, 24% on three or more nights a week, compared to 18% of men.
- Problems getting to sleep on three or more nights per week are particularly high under age 25, then decline slightly for men with age, but increase with age for women.
- Half of men and women over age 65 report sleep maintenance problems on three or more nights a week, compared to under a fifth of men and a third of women under 25.
- More men than women report that snoring or coughing disturbs their sleep, 30% of men and 20% of women more than once a week.
- Women are more likely to negatively rate their sleep quality, 26% compared to 20% of men.
- One in 10 people report taking sleeping medication on three or more nights a week (9% of men and 10% of women).

- 25% of women and 15% of men over 85 report taking sleeping medication on three or more nights a week.
- 14% of men and women working part-time sleep for more than eight hours per night, declining to about 6% of men and 10% of women for those working more than 30 hours per week, and remaining at this level even for people working very long hours (more than 48 hours per week).
- However, for people of both genders working long hours brings an increase in shorter sleep periods: 14% of women and 11% of men working more than 48 hours sleep less than six hours per night.
- Poor sleep quality is more frequently reported by long-hours workers and especially among women: 31% of long-hours women report poor sleep quality compared to only 23% of those who work 31-48 hours per week.
- Looking at these findings altogether suggests that the increase in shorter sleep periods for those working long hours is not only due to time constraints but other pressures such as stress.
- Only 6% of managers report more than eight hours sleep per night compared to 11% of those without managerial responsibilities.
- 14% of respondents least satisfied with their jobs reported regularly sleeping for less than six hours per night, compared with only 8% of those most satisfied with work.

Severe Osteoporoses Disorder

Scientists have identified a single mutated gene that causes Hajdu-Cheney syndrome, a disorder of the bones causing progressive bone loss and osteoporosis (fragile bones). The study, published in Nature Genetics March 6, gives vital insight into possible causes of osteoporosis and highlights the gene as a potential target for treating the condition.

There are only 50 reported cases of Hajdu-Cheney syndrome (HCS), of which severe osteoporosis is a main feature. Osteoporosis is a condition leading to reduction in bone strength and susceptibility to fractures. It is the most common bone disease, with one in two women and one in five men over 50 in the UK fracturing a bone because of the condition. This represents a major public health problem yet, until this study, possible genetic causes of osteoporosis were poorly understood.

The team of scientists, led by the National Institute for Health Research (NIHR) comprehensive Biomedical Research Centre (BRC) at King's College London and Guy's and St. Thomas, investigated the genetic cause of HCS in order to detect clues to the role genes might play in triggering osteoporosis.

53. Change Your Attitude for Your Happiness

Every person should always have the attitude to change oneself. Only if you adopt this concept of adaptability to the theme of changing your attitude it is only then that you are able to enjoy a happy life. If a person is strong headed and is never interested to listen about his attitude then such a person cannot be seen happy. Hence, always be flexible and then enjoy your life with full dose of happiness at your command.

Remez Sasson while giving his views on happiness feels that daily life can be made happier. It is a matter of choice. **It is our attitude that makes us feel happy or unhappy.** It is true, we meet all kinds of situations during the day, and some of them may not be conductive to happiness. We can choose to keep thinking about the unhappy events, and we can choose to refuse to think about them, and instead, relish the happy moments. All of us constantly go through various situations and circumstances, but we do not have to let them influence our reactions and feelings.

Talking about Happiness, Sasson feels that happiness is a feeling of inner peace and satisfaction. It is usually experienced when there are no worries, fears or obsessing thoughts, and this usually happens, when we do something we love to do or when we get, win, gain or achieve something that we value. It seems to be the outcome of positive events, but I actually comes from the inside, triggered by outer events. According to him some of the practical tips for increasing your happiness in your day to day daily life would be:-

1) Endeavor to change the way you look at things. Always look at the bright side. The mind may drag you to think about negativity and difficulties. Don't let it. Look at

the good and positive side of every situation.

2) Think of solutions, not problems.

3) Listen to relaxing, uplifting music.

4) Watch funny comedies that make you laugh.

5) Each day, devote some time to reading a few pages of an inspiring book or article.

6) Watch your thoughts. Whenever you catch yourself thinking negative thoughts, start thinking of pleasant things.

7) Always look at what you have done and not at what you haven't. Sometimes you may begin the day with the desire to accomplish several objectives. At the end of the day you might feel frustrated and unhappy, because you haven't been able to do all of those things.

Thus, it is your attitude which if changed on the basis of prevailing circumstances then it is instrumental in bringing your happiness.

54. Why Should You Enter Unhappiness Zone Due to Action of Someone Else

Be it a member of your family or a business associate or some relative and some words uttered by them or some of their action are such that unhappiness enters your life zone. Well, for all those who are intelligent people and for all those who would like to have happiness in their life, they should always remember a golden mantra and that is one should never permit action committed or performed by someone to result you're your unhappiness. Keep this in mind always and then you find that your life is not disturbed, your life is not perturbed due to action or non-action by someone.

During the course of my business and professional activities I remember the other day one gentleman started abusing me a lot on my telephone. I switched off the telephone but again after sometime this gentleman would not stop. He would continue all the rubbish nonsense talk on the phone. Very calmly and coolly I explained him the situation in the subject matter but still he was not interested to listen to whatever I was saying. A normal person in such a situation would get baffled, would become unhappy because of the action of that gentleman. But let me tell you that I was not baffled. I did not permit the action of speaking abusive language of that person enter my happiness zone and that is the reason I was happy mainly because of the fact that I was not disturbed at all mentally and emotionally with all that wrong and nonsense things being uttered by some other person. A week later this gentleman came to my house and expressed his apology for his abusive language over phone the other day. After a cup of tea with him I told him and explained to him that one should never get disturbed or perturbed just because of some action or some abusive language uttered by some other person. My dear readers, in your own life also if you accept this mantra, then it can become the happiness mantra for you to bring back your lost happiness and also it can be a formula to enable you to regain your happiness in your life specially if you adopt the concept of not getting disturbed, perturbed, abused due to actions of someone else.

The other day my friend and his wife when they had come to my place, told me that their daughter-in-law was making them unhappy.

They continued to say that the daughter in law would not allow their grandchildren to come and meet the grant parents and play with the grandparents. They continued further that this activity of the daughter-in-law was disturbing them, was making them unhappy and was making their life miserable. After listening to the whole story I calmly and coolly told them that look you for your own happiness you should never be disturbed with the action of someone else. I continued further to explain them that if your daughter-in-law does not bring your grand child closer to you, then it is definitely an activity with which you will be unhappy because the fact remains that every grandparent would love to play with their grandchildren, but the fact is that this activity should not be instrumental in taking away your happiness. I told him also that if you are just brooding every day on this point only, then lot of negativity would enter your mind zone which may not bring any positive results but at least it would be instrumental in providing unhappiness to you. Convinced with my arguments, the couple went home and when I met them after three weeks, I found that they were more cheerful in comparison with my previous meeting with them three weeks ago. Now, they continued to say that they were happy because they were not paying attention to this activity of the daughter in law of not allowing the grand children to meet the grand-parents. Likewise, while having a morning walk near our house, one of the morning walkers told me that, sir, I am very unhappy because my wife does not listen to me. So, every time when I see my wife, I get agitated and my happiness is vanished.

He continued to say that I am never happy specially when I am at home with my wife. I explained to him the real life mantra that let not unhappiness zone be created due to the action of someone else. In the initial stage the friend could not absorb what I wanted to say. But gradually, he adopted my concept and today they are very good couple because he has stopped thinking and talking about unhappiness in life even with the wrong and unjustifiable action of the wife. Ultimately the wife also pondered about her role plan in the family and when she found that even with the type of her role in the family, the husband was not at all feeling unhappy. She changed her way of life and the couple now is a very happy couple. Similarly, the other day while I was having professional consultation with a client of mine, I could see his wept eyes and the rolling tears coming therefrom.

Some ten minutes of intimate chat with him revealed that he was unhappy because the other day his own son aged 38 told him that look father you are the greatest fighter in the family. The fact is that when this type of hurting statements are made by some of our own family members whether right or wrong, we get disturbed. We get perturbed. Our happiness turns into unhappiness. We are tensed all the time. Well, in such situation and circumstances also if you want to be happy, then never ever the hurting statement and the action of someone destroy your happiness. Be happy and to be happy never take cognizance of the statement and the activity of someone else. Try to see what all you can do. But never be disturbed emotionally. Please do remember that if you are disturbed emotionally, you will be unhappy person and if you are unhappy person, surely you are going to get your health problems nearer to you.

In my seminar on retirement planning, I generally have emphasized that all persons specially who are going to retire if they want more happiness to come near to them in their old age, they should adopt Programme 3C for their wife. The 3C Programme which I have emphasized upon refers to Cash, Computer and Car for the spouse. I strongly believe that specially in the years to follow after your retirement, if your wife gets education about cash, namely the handling of the cash, the handling of the investment coupled with knowledge of computer so that in the old age when servants are not easily available, she can herself take care of booking of railway, airlines and other connected matters if she knows computer and finally if your spouse knows driving a car, then it can be a wonderful idea of happiness at the retirement time.

Thus, I strongly believe that if cash, computer and car become the companion of a married lady specially after the husband retires, then surely it will provide happiness in the family. Being inspired by this theme of mine, every year thousands of people throughout India take up this programme of 3C for their spouse.

However, the other day I met one participant in the seminar who said that this 3C formula is instrumental in bringing unhappiness in his life. I was really surprised. He narrated to me that when he told his wife to learn computer, the wife got angry and she said that you want me to learn computer so that you want to get lot of work of your office done by me.

The husband got really hurt because his objective of learning computer and car to the spouse was only to ensure that at times of necessity and in case of emergency the wife is equipped with modern gadgets including computer and car. But when the wife makes a statement that your making to learn computer is only with your sole benefit so that in my old age also, you want me to work very hard for you and you only want to save the salary of your computer operator.

When I heard this statement from this gentleman, I told him to be calm and quiet and advised him to let computer be taken away from his room and let the wife not understand the computer knowledge and let not the wife have any assignment of learning computer. Similarly, told him to let your wife be off from the leaning lesson of car driving.

However, after six months, the husband had a medical problem and there was a necessity to be admitted to the hospital immediately. At that point of time there was no other family member in the house. At that time the wife thought definitely it would help her better if she would have learnt car driving so that at the time of emergency and problem, she could drive the car to take the husband to the hospital. But please do remember that as far as you are concerned, preserving your happiness lies with you and that depends upon your action plan of not being attached with the actions of someone else.

Therefore, never let unhappiness enter your mind and body for the action or inaction of someone else.

If you want to keep some proposal in the family, then tell the benefits, explain the point of view but if they are not interested in your thinking, then let the world go as it goes.

Miracles of Health and Happiness

There is no reason that you should get yourself mentally disturbed about this type of situation. Also please do remember that if you are unhappy and if you are disturbed due to the actions of someone in the family, then your health problem also aggravates. This can even lead to depression and other health related diseases.

Therefore, to be happy be happy in all situations and one of the reasons through which you can avoid unhappiness is never to be attached to the theme of what others have told you or what is the reaction of one.

55. Inspire Lives of Others and Be Happy

One practical formula of deriving happiness which I have found in my own life is taking a resolution to inspire others and this one single thought will be instrumental in providing happiness to you. Take a look at last 20-30 years of your life when someone inspired you and the inspiration of someone has been responsible for uplifting your life. Hence, it is your sacred duty now to inspire the humanity at large and let your inspiration brings rays of hope in the lives of some people indeed.

Many times you feel that it is not possible for me to inspire someone else. I am not that a great person or that I am not that a rich man that I can inspire some other people in the community we live in. Never have this type of thought enter your mind. I strongly believe that every person in this world with God's grace has got so much power that he or she can inspire at least couple of people in the world. Hence, I want you to take a resolution to inspire at least a group of people in the community we live in. I also strongly believe that if you take up the task of inspiring some people at least, then your happiness definitely increases. I will like to share with my readers that I have taken a resolution to inspire at least one crore persons in the whole world in my life time. This may appear to be a big target. But I strongly feel with the blessings of the Almighty God and with the good wishes of all persons whom I meet I will definitely be able to achieve this target in my life. My aim is to inspire the humanity through my TV programme, through my writings, through my books, through my articles and through my talk shows happening in different parts of the world. It was in January 2011 I was speaking at a big gathering in Nagpur. At that time, the Commissioner of Income-tax who was the Chief Guest thereafter listening to my talk show clearly said that Mr. Lakhotia you will inspire not just crore people but you will inspire couple of crore people in the world. This type of statement coming from people at regular intervals inspires me again and again to do something more for the community we live in.

I want you, yes my dear readers, I want you to take a resolution to inspire 5, 10, 50 or more persons in your life time. In turn, as a return gift what I can give you is that you will enjoy immense happiness just by this act of inspiring others. Hence, the moral of the story is inspire others and be happy all the time.

My travel very regular indeed in different parts of India brings me in personal contact with lakhs of persons every year. I make it a point to inspire all whom I meet. This has now become a way of my life which I do enjoy. Last week I received a SMS on my mobile which read as under :- "Sir, your motivation, inspire me much, the result of which is that I am CA today to serve you better—CA Bhushan N. Toshniwal (Blind Student)." These types of message really provides me great happiness. I recollect that during my two previous seminars held at Pune I met Bhushan with his father. He is Blind but has great determination, the result of which is that today he is a qualified Chartered Accountant—I would invite all my readers to carry forward the good principles of motivating the people in different walks of our life at least for our own happiness.

56. The Thrilling Happiness

All along in this book we have been talking and discussing about various ways and means to experience the magic of health and happiness. The fact remains that happiness continues to be number one item on the agenda of almost all the human beings not just in India but in the whole world. It is this reason that we find that intelligent thinkers always think on something new which will provide greater happiness to them. It is also an accepted fact that money alone cannot buy happiness. It is also a reality that money is needed but money is required to make your better living standard.

But in any way money alone cannot be used as a tool to provide you happiness. It is time for you now to think about the thrilling happiness, the happiness which I see would give you a thrill in life. I want each and every reader of mine to experience and enjoy this thrilling happiness experience. But before we proceed to experience the thrilling happiness, what is needed is a desire, a keen desire in your heart to experience something innovative, something great which I call it as thrilling happiness. This concept of thrilling happiness is going to be something new which will aim at providing better quality of happiness for you. In initial stage what all you have to do is just try and think that yes you would also like to enjoy and experience the thrilling happiness in your life.

Once you keep this motto on your agenda book, then surely you will yourself come across some vistas and some situations which alone will be responsible for providing to you the thrilling happiness in your life. Also please do remember happiness is a continuous affair. Merely if you are happy one day, it does not mean that happiness will continue with you on an ever lasting basis. But I feel that if you can experience for yourself the thrilling experience of happiness (TEH), then surely your experience of this thrilling happiness will be stored in your heart, body and mind for the years to come. Hence, each and every human being should try to aim for achieving the thrilled happiness in ones life.

My experience is that you can experience thrilling happiness only when you are mentally and emotionally attached with the happiness. This is possible and this can become a reality only if you feel that you want to be attached both physically, emotionally, mentally with this type of experience of happiness. The well known fact is that we all get thrilled in our life whenever some great big occasion enters our door step. This occasion could be a big jump in your salary or a great big letter for your appointment in a big multinational organisation or it could even be when you find that a wonderful great marriage proposal has been received by you for your daughter. You are also thrilled when you find suddenly that a great big contract has been secured by you. Likewise, in social circle also a person feels thrilled when he finds that he has been elected as the President of the Chamber of Commerce or a Trade Organisation or a very big International Service Club Organisation. What we have discussed now is the thrill in life which may come near your door step once in a while. But end of the day I would like that we experience the thrilling happiness in our life. Merely getting a little bit more money or be awarded a big contract may definitely bring money for you but it may be instrumental in bringing a thrilling happiness experience for you. Hence, once if you feel that you would like to experience a thrilling experience of your life, then what is needed is some action, some activity or some thought which may not result into grabbing a little bit more share of money for you but what is required is an action or an occasion or an event or an item by doing which you get immense pleasure and that is known as the kingdom of thrilling experience. I also feel that if we are able to experience this thrilling experience of happiness in our life, then surely we will be able to keep in our almirah the memories of this thrilling happiness and in the years to come your today's thrilling happiness experience will be fresh only in your mind and even in your dreams. Well, we have talked a lot about the thrilling happiness but let us now try to see how to achieve this thrilling experience in reality. I remember the other day my friend Arvind was talking to me and he narrated to me a small little incident which happened while he was staying in Greater Kailash. Arvind said that his son Anshuman (grown up son who had just completed his schooling) had gone to a medical shop and had purchased some ointment basically a pain killer. The chemist at the medical shop said that the price was Rs. 89. Anshuman enquired whether there will be some concession or discount and no was the answer.

Anyway, Anshuman took the ointment and went home. A day later when his father Arvind was just glancing at the name and contents of this ointment, immediately his eyes went near the printed area on the ointment wherein the price of this ointment was mentioned. He found that the price mentioned was Rs. 159. The ointment was of a very reputed company. He immediately called Anshuman, his son and told look Anshuman, the other day you brought this ointment and you paid Rs. 89 to the chemist shop. But look here on the ointment the price mentioned is Rs. 159. Immediately just without answering any further questions Anshuman rushed immediately to the chemist shop and told the chemist that two days ago he had purchased this ointment and had paid Rs. 89 being the price asked by the chemist shop. Then Anshuman pointed his fingers on the price printed on the ointment box which says Rs. 159. Immediately Anshuman took out the balance money, handed over to the chemist and went home. A small little incident indeed but this small incident I am confident provided thrilling happiness to Arvind as well as to his Anshuman. When I came to know of this incident, I was having in my mind a replay of all that might have happened in respect of this incident between Arvind, Anshuman and the chemist shop. Dear readers, do remember that this type of small little activity and thing which happens in your life and which you handle with application of your mind and your soul, then arises the occasion when you can feel an experience for yourself of the thrilling happiness. Please do remember that it is not the quantum of money that will be responsible and instrumental in providing to you the thrilling happiness but it is this type of small little big activities which will help you to enjoy thrilling happiness. I remember the other day one old lady from E Block, Greater Kailash Part II, namely the colony next door telephoned me for a small little problem.

She said look Subhash we are just husband and wife staying in this 300 yard plot with a bungalow of their own. She continued further that she had a son staying in Sarita Vihar. I said fine, then what the problem is. She continued further and said that I had a daughter too and the daughter is staying out of India. She further continued that her son who stays in an apartment in Sarita Vihar has suggested that she sell this palatial house in Greater Kailash and that the parents move out from Greater Kailash to Sarita Vihar and stay with him. She wanted my comment and my thinking and my views in the above mentioned situation. I said madam, please tell me what is your desire and what is your wish. A frank confession was made by her that as the house in Greater Kailash was a big palatial house, she would like his son to stay in the house with full floor and she along with her husband would continue to occupy another floor and that she was not feeling happy and comfortable to go and stay in an apartment in Sarita Vihar. Realizing her desire, upon realising her desire, I told her that it would be better to tell the son to shift from Sarita Vihar to Greater Kailash and as they would be staying on seperate floors, both children and parents would be able to have the desire space.

I further continued to say that in your old age if the son and his family were to stay in the Greater Kailash building in which the parents are staying, it will provide emotional satisfaction and strength to the parents specially keeping in view their old age. She communicated my message to his son. This was about six months ago. Last week she telephoned me again and said that unfortunately her husband had expired but in view of my thinking and suggestion to her, the husband has made a WILL exclusively in the name of the wife with full freedom to deal the property in the manner as she would like to do for this property. Although this lady was unhappy with heavy heart due to the demise of her husband but nevertheless she said that she was feeling very happy, satisfied and tension free because of my advice. She continued further that she would now prepare her WILL and give away the big Greater Kailash palatial house property to the son and the daughter in equal proportion. She wanted that her property should be given to the children not right now on day one but only after her demise so that she is able to live as she would like to live. My endorsement was okayed on her thinking. I advised to her that her action plan was perfectly in order and that she was competent to prepare a WILL in respect of the property she inherited from her late husband and that in the WILL she was also fully competent to pass on her property only after her death to the children namely the son as well as the daughter in equal proportion. I also suggested her that, Madam looking into the problem which might come up in the years to come the best course would be to get the WILL registered. She acted on my advice and the other day she came to meet me with a big bunch of flowers expressing her happiness on my advice. This was a moment of my own thrilling happiness and I was feeling so very happy because my advice granted peace, solace and happiness to someone, then definitely it was a moment for me to be thrilled. Just for five to ten minutes a small little chat over the phone I do not charge any professional fee and today I was feeling still happy because by seeing the happy face of this old lady I was getting immense happiness to me and this I call it an example of thrilling happiness. Similar is also the situation of another client of mine who is 95 years of age and his wife may be about 89 years.

This couple has great faith on the advice being given to them by me specially relating to succession planning and other connected matters. I am thrilled that I find that this young man of 95 years comes along with his wife and in my chamber tells me that look Subhash if I go at any point of time, my wife is totally dependent on your advice, your guidance and your suggestions. When I listen to this statement, a sense of thrilling happiness enters my mind, body and soul zones and I find the thrilling happiness because if an action by me can bring happiness in the life of someone else and that happiness when I experience and see of these people, I am really thrilled and for me it becomes not merely happiness formula but a thrilling happiness formula. Fortunately or unfortunately my work is such that I come in contact with a large number of people whether as my client or whether as the listeners in my seminars and talk shows in different parts of India and abroad, but the experience of thrilling happiness is enjoyed by me very often as I continue my journey guiding and helping a large section of the Indian population in particular on all aspects connected with investment planning, the tax planning, the practical life planning relating to investment and such other connected matters.

The other day a middle aged couple entered my office with a very grim look. They were middle aged as I said but from their face they appeared to be very old and the main reason of their looking much more than their age was the big problems which they faced in their life mainly because of personal guarantee given by the husband to the bank which resulted into closure of various business activities and finally his wife received a big tax demand from the tax officer amounting to little more than rupees 40 to 50 lakhs. When they entered my room, they could not not speak for a few minutes. They were unable to explain what their problem was. The wife started crying and crying like a child. I consoled them. I tried to understand their problem. And then I tried to help them in all possible manner that I could do. Six months later one fine morning I found they again entered my office but with a smiling face and looking at least 15 years younger. Without uttering a single word their face was communicating me the happiness which they were enjoying. They were happy because they had won the tax matter and their worries and tensions were completely over. The happiness which I could see on their faces brought for me my thrilling happiness. Similarly, two brothers carrying on business together suddenly one day one brother became ill, hospitalised, liver transplant was in progress but in between this brother expired. His widow was just a house wife, not knowing much about tax and investment and the worldly affairs and no other relative to help them. She had no brother. But she just had an old father who himself was 85. She came to me, told the problem and she knew no route to overcome the problems and handle the situation consequent to death of her husband. I tried to solve her problem and merely after an hour chat I found that the lost happiness on her face came back. She was happy at least because of the fact that she was able to save the money left by the husband which was in a shattered situation and that she was able to settle her account with the brother-in-law. Now this widow lives peacefully with her young son and has adjusted her life in the given circumstances. When I think about this incident sitting in cool, leisure hours of mine, I find a sort of thrilling happiness experienced by me because I feel that with God's grace I was able to complete the task of providing some assistance, some help to someone at real crisis time. I feel that if at any point of time in your life whether in your business or in profession or whether as a retired person or as a student, if you are able to render some activities with non-selfish motives in mind and which could be instrumental to bring some happiness to someone, then surely in turn you will receive the thrilling happiness experience for you. It is time now for you first of all to accept this concept of thrilling happiness and then aim at achieving your thrilling experience the memories of which will continue providing to you even in future your thrilling happiness the moment when you remember your golden past.

Live as you like, work what you want to do, be what you like, be what you want to be, these are really a great big luxuries of life. Those who can achieve these luxuries, they will be able to have an experience of thrilling happiness in their life. Hence, if you want to experience an example of thrilling happiness for you, then it is time now for you to think what you are doing, to think what you want to do, to think what you like to be and then after thinking, meditating, applying your mind, take a decision and start finally your journey when you can say proudly that yes you are living in the manner as you would like to live and you are doing that money earning activity which you want to do and this answer when you get will definitely provide a great satisfaction to you and would be instrumental in making available an experience of thrilling happiness for you.

Finally, do remember that your thrilling happiness which can become reality come true in your life with some little activities of your life will surely provide you an everlasting experience of thrilling happiness.

57. Rainbow Tips on Health and Happiness

The following are some of the rainbow points for your Health & Happiness. It is expected that all these pointers will surely help you to have your robust health coupled with a big bag of happiness for your.

Your Happiness Is an Inside Job

You may be rich or famous but merely being rich or famous does not mean that you would surely be a very happy person. American research conducted long back may be over a decade ago has revealed that happiness has no correlation with reference to social status of an individual or his income more the gender and not the slain colour of a person. The National Opinion Research Centre (NORC) in Chicago, for instance, has been surveying people on their feelings of well-being since 1957. They found that 30 percent of people now describe themselves as "very happy," compared with 35 percent in 1957! The clincher: Americans now make twice as much money! About a decode ago the results from a worldwide survey revealed that Bangladeshis are the happiest people on earth. Apparently, once basic needs (food, clothing, shelter) are satisfied, happiness does not increase in proportion with the amount of money you have.

So if money's not the key, what is? Personality, say psychologists at Fordham University in New York City. The devastating impact that events can have on you—whether it's a job loss or the death of a loved one—really depends on your ability to learn to observe your reactions and improve your perspective from the inside out.

Feel Contended and Healthy for Your Happiness

The fact remains that good health alone cannot bring happiness in life. However, in case you are contended in life then surely more happiness you will be able to experience. In fact, a 1991 study conducted at the University of Amsterdam in the Netherlands found that people who were severely ill yet content with their lives considered themselves only slightly less happy than people with no real health problems. What's even more interesting is that researchers have found that people who regularly experience a lot of negative emotions tend to recall their health as being worse than it actually was. In other words, If you're feeling rotten about life, you may be recalling stomach aches that never really happened.

Judge Your Happiness By Verifying How Satisfied Are You

If you are satisfied in life then the chances are that you would be a happy person. The more you are satisfied the more happy person you would be. Nearly a decade ago I had found in a health news magazine a small little quiz which will enable a person to me the level of his satisfaction. I feel that even today this quiz could be of help to enable you to judge the level of your satisfaction. Take this one-minute quiz to find out just how content you really are. Rate each statement according to the scale below. Remember, be honest.

7 – Strongly agree

6 – Agree

5 – Slightly agree

4 – Neither agree nor disagree

3 – Slightly disagree

2 – Disagree

1 – Strongly disagree

_____ In most ways, my life is close to my ideal.
_____ The conditions of my life are excellent.
_____ I am satisfied with my life.
_____ So far, I have gotten the important things I want in life.
_____ If I could live my life over, I would change almost nothing.

Add your score to see if you are:

35 to 31   - Extremely satisfied
26 to 30   - Satisfied
21 to 25   - Slightly satisfied
20   - Neutral
15 to 19   - Slightly dissatisfied
10 to 14   - Dissatisfied
5 to 9   - Extremely dissatisfied

Go Religious to Be More Happy

Accepted fact is that if you continue your religious regular relationship either with a Church or Temple or Gurudwara or a Mosque then your happiness level will be higher. About a decade ago a poll of 32,000 people in U.S. found that 45 percent of those who attended religious services several times a week described themselves as being "very happy" while only 25 percent of those who attended less than once a month considered themselves to be "very happy."

It may be that prayers encourage people to develop a hopeful attitude. Or it may be that religious singing, chanting, meditation, and dance quiets a harassed mind and fosters joy.

Keep Away the Joy Killers to Be Happy

Sadhu J.P. Vaswani feels that one should keep away all the joy killers from yourself. Well, then the question may arise in your mind as to what these joy killers are. Well, according to Sadhu Vaswani the following joy killers should always be kept in mind and one should keep away from them:-

(a) Hate: Hatred is like fire. So long as fire burns within you, you cannot have joy in life. When a thought of hatred comes to you, trample it and breathe out a thought of love and goodwill.

(b) Resentment: So long as we have feeling of resentment within us, we do not and cannot, get joy of life. Our daily life is full of little irritations, which cause resentment. This is what keeps us away from the joy.

(c) Fear: It has rightly been said that there is no medicine for fear. To have real joy of life, we must develop the spirit of fearlessness. It is courage that comes to the rescue of a man in times of danger. It is said that 'He, who loss wealth, loses much; he, who loses a friend, loses more; but he who loses courage, loses all.'

Hence, if you keep the above joy killers at a distance then you would enjoy better happiness in your life. Sadhu Vaswani also feels that one should also develop the habit of not thinking and not talking negatively at least for your own bliss and happiness.

Cancer Update from Johns Hopkins

Here is a latest update from Johns Hopkins who tells the world that there is an alternative way to Cancer Care. Hopkins feels that every person has cancer cells in the body. These cancer cells do not show up in the standard tests until they have multiplied to a few billion. When doctors tell cancer patients that there are no more cancer cells in their bodies after treatment, it just means the tests are unable to detect the cancer cells because they have not reached the detectable size.

Cancer cells occur between 6 to more than 10 times in a person's lifetime. To overcome the multiple nutritional deficiencies, changing diet and including supplements will strengthen the immune system. He goes on to say that Chemotherapy involves poisoning the rapidly-growing cancer cells and also destroys rapidly-growing healthy cells in the bone marrow, gastrointestinal tract etc, and can cause organ damage, like liver, kidneys, heart, lunges, etc. Radiation while destroying cancer cells also burns, scars and damages healthy cells, tissues and organs. Initial treatment with chemotherapy and radiation will often reduce tumor size. However, prolonged use of chemotherapy and radiation do not result in more tumor destruction. An effective way to battle cancer is to starve the cancer cells by not feeding it with the foods it needs to multiply.

Finally, Hopkins feels very strongly that Sugar is a cancer-feeder. By cutting off sugar it cuts off one important food supply to the cancer cells. Sugar substitutes like NutraSweet, Equal, Spoonful, etc. are made with Aspartame and it is harmful. A better natural substitute would be Manuka honey or molasses but only in very small amounts. Table salt has a chemical added to make it white in colour. Better Alternative is Bragg's aminos or sea sale.

Milk causes the body to produce mucus, especially in the gastrointestinal tract. Cancer feeds on mucus. By cutting off milk and substituting with unsweetened soy milk, cancer cells are being starved.

Cancer cells thrive in an acid environment. A meat-based diet is acidic and it is best to eat fish, and a little chicken rather then beef or pork. Meat also contains livestock antibiotics, growth hormones and parasites, which are all harmful, especially to people with cancer. A diet made of 80% fresh vegetable and juice, whole grains, seeds, nuts and a little fruits help put the body into an alkaline environment. About 20% can be from cooked food including beans. Fresh vegetable juices provide live enzymes that are easily absorbed and reach down to cellular levels within 15 minutes to nourish and enhance growth of healthy cells. To obtain live enzymes for building healthy cells try and drink fresh vegetable juice (most vegetables including bean sprouts) and eat some raw vegetables 2 or 3 times a day. Avoid coffee, tea and chocolate, which have high caffeine. Green tea is a better alternative and has cancer-fighting properties. Water-best to drink purified water, or filtered, to avoid known toxins and heavy metals in tap water. Distilled water is acidic, avoid it.

Hopkins also feels that Cancer is a disease of the mind, body and spirit. A proactive and positive spirit will help the cancer warrior be a survivor. Anger, unforgiveness and bitterness put the body into a stressful and acidic environment. Learn to have a loving and forgiving spirit. Learn to relax and enjoy life.

The above mentioned details relating to new Cancer thinking were sent to me by our family friend Dr. Rajaram Jaipuria, a leading industrialist based in Delhi with a note that the above subject matter on Cancer should be Zeroxed and send to anyone important in our life. I feel that circulating important reading material to someone you love would provide you happiness.

Laughter for Your Health

Let laugher be a part of your daily life if you want to be healthy. A leading child paediatrician by the name of Dr. Joachim Gardemann while writing prescriptions to his patients would write a specific advise telling his patients to laugh and laugh for better health. He strongly feels that we really have to encourage laughing and being happy because it is one of mankind's most health promoting resources. I remember to have read long back in a magazine entitled — Longevity & Health that in Germany even a decade ago there were more than 20 professional clinic clowns whose job is to cheer up such young patients although there has been little in the way to empirical study about the benefits.

That occurred to Sherry Hiber in 1998, when she was helping to produce television sitcoms in the United States and often saw members of the audience convulsed in laughter. "I used to see the people go out at the end of the show and thought to myself 'perhaps for the rest of the night something interesting will be going on in their bodies." She started to plough through specialist books on the topic but came across little more than a few anecdotes and some contradictory small-scale studies. Afterwards, she made up her mind to start a unique project called RX Laughter and enlisted the support of medical experts from the University of California. The comedy health advocates have their own homepage at www.rxlaughter.org.

At one of the conference organised by the American College of Cardiology the scientists were of the view that stress in life cause 35% less blood circulation while laughing increase blood circulation by 22%. As per a research by Dr. Mischel Miller during one week if a person resorts to 30 minutes exercise for three days and laughs at least 15 minutes a day then his heart will be in tip top condition. Unfortunately most of us have forgotten to laugh but when we accept the fact that laughing is a wonderful health pill then we all should make laughing a way of life and a daily routine. If you feel shy to laugh alone then start laughing in a group. I have designed a special recipe which is practical and which would help you to laugh alone. Well, the recipe is simple and easy to adopt. Here it is. Close your room. Let there be no one in the room except you. Now, lock the room. Play the music in top volume. Now, while the music is being played on a high pitch you start a big loud laugh. Laugh non stop. Laugh for 10 to 15 minutes daily. Implement this formula on a daily basis. Compare your face just after 15 days. You will be able to experience the healthy benefits of laughing and a new glow on your face. Implement this simple formula and tell this recipe for laughter to your friends and relatives and do write to me your experience at slakhotia@satyam.net.in.

Say Good-bye to Anger for Your Health

If you care for your health then it is time now to say good bye to "Anger." This is what happens when we are angry:-

- The brain tells the body to pump out the action-hormone nor-adrenaline.
- Breathing deepens, the heart beats more rapidly, blood pressure arises, and pupils dilate.
- Blood is diverted from other organs to the heart, central nervous system, and muscles.
- Digestion is suspended, glucose levels rise, men have a testosterone boost. You're on red alert.
- You clench you fist, teeth, colon.

Anger is the body's natural emotional and physical response to being threatened, says Gael Lindenfield, author of Managing Anger. "It's one of the first emotions we experience as babies, when Mum isn't as forthcoming with the milk as we'd want." According to some experts many of us are addicted to the highs we experience when the body releases nor-adrenaline, the hormone which kick-start us into action, by mobilising fatty acids from the body's fat deposits.

Please do remember that your anger may result into anxiety, detachment in life, high level of blood pressure, asthma, phobias, hysterias, weight problem, gas problem, insomnia, sexual dysfunctions. Thus, more than one ailments corner you just because of anger, hence, avoid anger at every cost.

Prayers Helps You to Get Your Happiness

Prayers are your passport for perfect happiness. I remember to have read fifteen years ago in The Readers Digest that lady by the name of Imi Rumpp stopped praying for a winning lottery ticket years ago. With a husband, two kids and a full-time job, she didn't have time for trivial pursuits. But when she learned that her sister Miki needed a kidney transplant, Mimi began praying for a donor. This, she thought, is worth praying for. Less than a year later Miki has a new kidney, courtesy of a woman who heard of Miki's plight and was so moved that she had herself tested; she was a perfect match. Coincidence? Luck? Divine intervention? Rumpp is sure: "It was a miracle." The actual life story of Mimi Rumpp would surely convince most of my readers about the great miracle powers of prayers. I personally have great faith in the healing powers of prayers. Once a special survey was conducted by Newsweek which gave a finding based on facts that 54% of the adults say that they pray while the survey said that 29% of the persons who participated in the survey said that they prayed every day. A very special result of the survey was that 87% of the people who were surveyed were firmly of the view that believed that the God answers their prayers while just about 15% people said that they had lost faith in the prayers because God had not answered their prayers. If you have faith in prayers then start praying on a regular basis. Do remember that faith is a powerful medicine, hence have faith in prayers and pray and relax.

Jimmy Carter, the former President of USA used to say that he would "Pray" many times a day and that he had great sense of peace as a result of these prayers.

My definition of "PRAYER" contains in the following lines which I read somewhere and I liked it and so I am reproducing the same for the benefit of my readers:

- Prayer is talking to God.
- Prayer is listening to God.
- Prayer is being quiet with God.
- Prayer is learning to think the thoughts of God.
- Prayer is learning to speak the words of God.
- Prayer is learning to do the deeds of God.
- Prayer is understanding the power and wisdom of God in nature.
- Prayer is understanding the love and mercy of God in human experience.
- Prayer is believing God.
- Prayer is trusting God.
- Prayer is resting on the promises of God.
- Prayer is becoming identified with God.
- Prayer is being committed with God.
- Prayer is working with God.
- Prayer is waiting with God.
- Prayer is conquering with God.
- Prayer is praise and thanksgiving.
- Prayer is joy and assurance.
- Prayer is being at peace with God.

Some think of prayer as something to do. A rite. A routine. A spiritual chore. Actually, prayer is a way of life.

Be Spiritual, Be Healthy and Happy

If you are spiritual then you will be more healthy and only when you are healthy then you are bound to the happy. Dr. Harold G. Koenig, director of the Duke University Centre for the Study of Religion, Spirituality and Health in Durham, NC, says, "For many years, scientists thought spirituality was something only neurotic people pursued. But now we're finding evidence that may be spirituality is part of what it is to be human, and that it may work together with our individual psychology to indirectly affect our health."

Dr. Koenig's statement is based on the findings of the research conducted by the Centre. In a study of 87 seriously depressed men and women, it was found that those who were spiritually centred recovered 70 percent faster than those who weren't. In yet another study involving 1,700 people over the age of 65 it was found that those who attended religious services had a significantly stronger immune system that those who did not.

It is also interesting to note that more than one hundred medical schools in USA offer special courses on spirituality and health. Now, even the Doctors all over the world have started accepting that all those persons who are spiritual they are more heartier and they heal also fast and such persons are less likely to die prematurely than non believers in Spirituality.

More Than Two Drinks a Day Bring the Risk of Cancer

About one in 10 cancers in men and one in 33 in women in western European countries are caused by current and past alcohol consumption, according to study released in April, 2011.

For some type of cancer, the rates are significantly higher, it said. In 2008, for men, 44,25 and 33% of upper digestive track, liver and colon cancers respectively were caused by alcohol in six of the countries examined, the study found.

The countries were UK, Italy, Spain, Greece, Germany and Denmark. The study also showed that half of these cancer cases occurred in men who drank more than a recommended daily limit of 24 grammes of alcohol, roughly two small glasses of wine or a pint of beer.

The cancer rates for women in the same countries, along with the Netherlands and France, was 18 percent for throat, mouth and stomach, 17 percent for liver, 5 percent for breast and 4 percent for colon cancer. Four-fifths of these cases were due to daily consumption above recommended limits, set for women at half the level of men.

The International Agency for Research on Cancer has long maintained that there is a causal link between alcohol consumption and cancers, especially of the liver, colon, upper digestive tract and, for women, breast. "Our data show that many cancer cases could have been avoided if alcohol consumption is limited to two alcoholic drinks per day in men and one alcoholic drink per day in women," said Madlen Schutze, lead author of the study. My personal view however, is that at least for your own health the best course would be to do away with hard drinks — completely and for ever. If you cannot accept this advice of mine then at least get to the above advice which is scientific and with a logic.

Recipe for a Full Happy Year

Here is a wonderful recipe for a full month period as sent to me by a friend of mine. I am sure you would enjoy also.

Take 12 completed months. Clean them carefully of all bitterness, hate and envy. Cut each month into 29,30 or 31 different pieces, but do not cook them all at the same time. Prepare one day at a time, with the following ingredients: A pinch of faith, a pinch of patience, a pinch of courage and a pinch of work. Add to each day one part hope, faithfulness and kindness. Mix well with one part prayer, one part meditation and one part application. Season with a portion of god spirits, a pinch of happiness, a little action and a good measure of humour. Place everything in a vessel of love. Cook well on the fire of radiant happiness. Garnish with a smile and serve abundantly.

Control Your Anger to Achieve Your Happiness

If you are able to achieve control over the unfortunate passion of anger you will find that your family life, your social life, your business life and above all your spiritual life will be a real blissful one. Everyday of the year every hour of the day and every minute of the hour you will experience bliss, happiness, cheerfulness just if you throw away anger permanently. The enthusiasm which is present amongst you has deteriorated and fallen out because of anger getting control over your enthusiasm. It is high time that you bring back the lost enthusiasm and vitality in you just by controlling the anger. Finally, do write your personal "Daily Diary" every day. Mahatma Gandhi has written a number of times about the utility of writing a daily diary. In this "Daily Diary" write as to how many times you became angry today. Read the diary everyday and then you will find that you are yourself ashamed of for being angry on small little points the whole day. This is how you can avoid your habit of becoming angry. Do remember everything is possible in this world only when your purpose of achieving that is really strong worded. Hence, if you are interested to control the anger enemy then it is high time that you start right now and stop becoming angry. Do think once in a while the bad effects on your health, wealth and family just by being angry. Also you will see that from day one your life will be real blissful one once your anger habit has gone out of your action plan of the day.

That is why the man who becomes angry never does a great amount of work, and the man whom nothing can make angry accomplish so much. The man who gives way to anger, or hatred, or any other passion cannot work; he only bridges himself to peace and does nothing practical. It is the calm, forgiving equitable, well balanced mind that does that greatest amount of work. This was what Swami Vivekananda spoke at London on 10th November, 1896 while delivering a talk on practical Vedanta. This statement which was delivered by Swami Vivekananda more than a century ago still holds good and valid for the present generation the world over. All sensible persons should ponder as to why we cannot remain calm and quite and why we should express our anger when there is an occasion to become angry but at that occasion if a person does not become angry that would be the real achievement of life. If a person were to dismantle his habit of becoming angry and wins over the attitude of being angry you will find that such a person would find this world a better place to live in. Let us travel in the wonderland of calmness because it is the calmness of the mind which will bring in cheerfulness and freshness the whole day in comparison with the person who is carrying on his daily routine in an angry mood.

The habit of being calm and quiet can be achieved by you if in the first instance you sit down in an isolated place and pray to God to grant you strength so that you can control your anger and then you can be calm and quiet. Yes, if real dedication is there for the purpose of controlling your anger it is really possible to control your anger without any difficulty.

When you have started dealing with worldly affairs without the help of anger you will find that this world is a better place to live in. Your day-to-day activities which are now carried on by you without support of anger will bring in better health, happiness and all-round cheerfulness to you. In your workplace in your family life and in all the walks of life you will find that removing anger from your dictionary will mean the real enjoyment of the bliss of your life. Your bowels will be moving correctly and you will have no gastric trouble and you will find that your small ailments, the gastric trouble and the other little health problems are all due to the fact that we carry on the day-to-day activities of the world with anger on our top of the list. The first step in control of the anger lies in just thinking every day that I will control my mind and I will not get angry under any circumstances.

Never Argue for Your Own Happiness

Never argue at least for your happiness. Never enter into an argument. Why do you want to win an argument? It offers you no tangible benefit. It will only inflate your ego, wound the other man and lead to friction between friends. Let the other man hold his opinion. There are incorrigible idiols in this world who can never be converted, who can never be made to see sense. Do not waste your time and breath on them. You will only suffer exhaustion and earn enmity. This paragraph I had read somewhere. Where and when I do not remember but the fact is that after reading it once I feel like reading it again and again. It has given me great strength to develop for me the habit of "no argument."

When you Argue you only try to satisfy the dormant ego within your body. Let not the habit of argument be under the undue influence of your ego, otherwise you are going to be an unhappy man, a man full of ailments and your "dynamic personality" will be reduced to "no-personality." If you constantly argue to win over an argument you would only end up in winning the argument then just think what effectively have you won. It is just the winning of your ego over your brain thinking process.

Reversely if you lose an argument you are pale and not gay for the whole day. Why then argue?

Mother-in-law versus daughter-in-law, or father versus son or finally husband versus the wife are the main groups which are the targets of the bad after effects coming to you and your body as a result of arguments. Enjoy bliss and happiness and so never argue. The bliss of inner peace you too can experience only if you were to take an vow as to never "argue" at any point of time. The family never splits, the married life does not lead to divorce and finally the business partnership does not result into dissolution but only when we resort to the theme of maintaining the habit of giving up "argument." You can always express your point of view to the other party but never ever attempt to win the argument — it never pays specially in the long run.

Health Juices for Your Vibrant Health

These days whether young or old everyone is concerned about his health. It is only when a man becomes ill, then he realises that the first lesson of happiness is good health. Science has proved beyond doubt that consuming a lot of fresh juices and fresh fruits & vegetables results into robust health both for male and female.

Carrot juice which is a full of Vitamin-E is one of the best juice to develop immunity and strength of the body. Carrot juice if taken in the morning on empty stomach is really very beneficial. Those persons who would like to prepare a "Juice Cocktail" can add spinach to the carrot juice thereby special cocktail drink of fresh juice is ready to bring health & vitality for you.

World famous food scientist Benzamin Galelord Hauserhad had pioneered raw juice therapy. Similarly, Dr. M.W. Walker the author of a famous book entitled "Raw Vegetable Juices" remained healthy even at the age of 111 years.

It is no good to drink tea or coffee. Instead a person can take fresh "Basil Juice (Tulsi)" together with ginger and hot water. A little milk and jaggery if added to this basil ginger juice then it makes a wonderful health drink. It is very well known fact that basil possesses many medicinal properties which help develop memory. Hence, it is equally good for young school going children.

For persons suffering from indigestion they can take the Mint juice (pudina juice). To make the mint juice tasty a person can add lemon and honey.

If Ginger juice alone is taken with a small quantity of mineral salt it would help in removing the cough and cold. The ginger juice would be equally wonderful juice for persons suffering from Asthma.

If a person wants to remain healthy and cheerful he should try to increase his intake of fruits and vegetables so that after developing fruit habit the ideal healthy man should change his food habit whereby his food should constitute up to 80% by way of fruits and vegetables alone and rest 20% can be normal daily diet.

Those persons suffering constipation may take the orange juice early in the morning. The orange juice is surely going to correct the constipation. The orange juice can be taken once or twice in a day. From the point of view of health Emblica juice (Amla juice) is the best of all the juices which contains the richest source of Vitamin-C. Amla juice helps in maintaining strength in the old age and brings new vitality, vigour and strength. It would be wonderful to have juice of fresh two Amlas every day in the morning which will surely prevent ageing of a person. Little honey can be added to this Amla juice. Pineapple juice is also very rich in Vitamin-C. It also contains Vitamins A & B. It is better if nothing is taken for at least 2 to 3 hours after consuming the Pineapple juice.

For many of the readers it may be a news but the fact is that potato juice is also very rich in Vitamin-C. The potato juice can be derived from the potato by putting it in juicer and extracting juice therefrom. Tomato juice is equally wonderful juice drink because it contains a lot of iron. Tomato juice is very rich in Vitamin A, B & Vitamin-C. It is better to consume Tomato juice than Tomato soup. Tomato juice and Apple juice of equal quantity can be mixed together with a tea spoon of honey to make a real tasty juice cocktail. Similarly, together with Tomato juice and juice of Carrot and the juice of Spinach can be mixed to bring yet another wonderful cocktail drink. Avoid drinking aerated water and better go in for these type of cocktails and mocktails. Cabbage and Carrot juice can be mixed together so also Spinach. Thus, yet another cocktail drink can be prepared at home by putting in cabbage juice, Carrot juice and Spinach juice.

A wonderful health drink can be prepared with fresh Spinach juice and a little of jaggery.

In the morning with empty stomach if fresh wheat grass juice is consumed it provides a wonderful drink. This is really very good for anemic persons and helps in generating more blood in the body.

Road to Happiness

The following happiness formula of Mac Anderson and B.J. Gallagher has inspired me. This is exactly what he writes:

"When I travel on business, I like to talk to the taxi drivers who take me from the airport to my hotel, or to a convention centre, or to a restaurant. Taxi drivers are often immigrants with interesting personal histories and unusual cultural background. I ask them how long they've been in America, how they chose which city to live in, and what they like best about where they live. Of course, I also ask them for advice on good local restaurants and any special attractions they'd recommend to a visitor. I've had some great experiences on my travels, thanks to the advice of tax drivers! On one trip about ten years ago, I was making conversation with the taxi driver, asking him my usual questions about how he came to live where he lived. Then I asked him a hypothetical question: "If you could live anywhere in the world—and if money was no object—where would you live?"

Without hesitating even for a second, he replied, " I live in my heart. So, it really doesn't matter where my body lives. If I am happy inside, then I live in paradise, no matter where my residence is."

I felt humbled and a little foolish for my question. Of course he was right—happiness is an inside job. He had reminded me of something I already knew, but had forgotten. If you can't find happiness inside yourself, you'll never find it in the outside world, no matter where you move. Wherever you go, there you are. You take yourself with you. I am grateful for the wisdom of that taxi driver. And I'm grateful for all the wisdom others have shared with me about how to be happy.

It is Time to Take Care of Your Happiness

"You have to take care of your happiness" says Celine Dion the world famous singer of Titanic fame. The loved and real popular singer which is evident from the fact that over 130 million albums of her have been sold world wide.

Besides, she has won five Grammys. Dion said the above punch line when she was talking to a columnist for an exclusive Reader's Digest interview which got published in July, 2002. If we really want happiness in life, we must really think and rethink what Dion has felt in life namely — that it is you and you alone who have to take care of your own happiness. If you really want to be happy, then in the first stage always remember that our own tender care for happiness will bring happiness for us. The set back to getting happiness is only when you depend on outside agencies to provide you with your share of happiness. Swami Chidananda a senior monk in charge of Vivekananda Vedanta Society of Chicago says that as good and evil coexist, happiness and suffering exist at all time in this world and as long as life is there on earth, suffering is going to stay. This is the reality of life, which we should also accept. Acceptance of this reality will help us to bring happiness close to our heart. Analysing the root cause of unhappiness Swami Chidananda says that it is because we don't know our true self, which is pure awareness beyond the body and mind, we suffer seeking to find happiness in the external world.

The real happiness is all contained in our inner self only. This I feel should be accepted as the proved reality based on the age old dictum contained in our scripture "GITA (6.5)" which was propounded centuries ago. Swami Chidananda says that happiness and unhappiness come and go and we need not blame the world for this for no amount of material prosperity or success in worldly dealings can give us real joy; they give only comfort and facilities. If we get closer and closer to our own real self, we come closer to happiness and bliss. The other day a newspaper report appeared which stated that on old man of 75 years lost his son in the first place, then lost his entire left over savings of Rs. 4,000. This man lived near Jamnagar, Gujarat. His only son aged 25 years had just started a small business of cloth after utilising the entire capital of his father. Business was going on as usual. Six month's back five-six people from Mathura came to meet his son and gave him the offer to come over to Mathura where there was good demand of cloth from Gujarat. The son got in the trap of making quick money and left for Mathura but did not return to village for six months. His father, being worried, collected all his balance life savings of Rs. 4,000 and proceeded to hunt for his son at Mathura. At the Mathura Station, his entire money of Rs. 4,000 was pick pocketed by some one. He could not find his son. He was weeping. Suddenly some representatives of recently framed organisation — Indian Welfare Society came in and they fed this old man and gave him money to return to his village. Just imagine the vast quantum of happiness which the representatives of this organisation might have experienced by rendering small little help to the old man. You and I in this trouble filled world if were to extend similar unsolicited help and assistance to those who need them, then we would experience the real happiness, which we have been looking for here and there but could not find it.

Spiritual Happiness with Chappal Distribution

The other day while I was delivering a talk on Health & Happiness at a local Rotary Club in Delhi, one member of the Rotary Club narrated his actual life experience which provided him exceptional happiness and bliss. One day this Gentleman was standing on a road, it was a very hot day, he saw a poor person on the road with no shoes or Chappal. A little later he saw this poor person going near the road side cobbler and just staring at the shoes and Chappals which were in the cobbler's shop for repairs.

Suddenly, this Gentleman got an idea. He purchased one set of Chappals from the local nearby market and presented it to this person who did not have Chappals and was walking on the streets of Delhi in the hot weather. The person presenting the Chappals was really surprised when he found that the poor person who received the set of Chappals from him was just weeping and crying out of sheer joy. By distributing just one set of Chappals to a real poor and needy person the person who had presented this set of Chappals found that this one small act of service to the humanity provided him immense happiness and bliss. Now, this Gentleman distributes free Chappals and shoes every year. A real life story really providing one tip for enjoying the happiness and bliss.

Take Time to Think and Be Happy

These days everyone is busy. No one has time. I feel that if we have time to think then we can become more happy. Recently my childhood friend sent me the following lines, a reading of the same gives me some strength for my happiness. Here it is:

>Take time to think.
>It is the source of power.
>Take time to play.
>It is the secret of perpetual youth.
>Take time to read.
>It is the fountain of wisdom.
>Take time to pray.
>It is the greatest power on earth.
>Take time to love and be loved.
>It is a God-given privilege.
>Take time to be friendly.

It is the road to happiness.
Take time to laugh.
It is the music of the soul.
Take time to give.
It is too short a day to be selfish.
Take time to work.
It is the price of success.
Take time to do charity.
It is the key to heaven.

The Happiness Keys of Wisener

The times of India dated 15th February, 2004 contained a very interesting write up on Ten keys of Happiness by Christian Wisener which are as under:

➤ Listen to your body's wisdom, which expresses itself through signals of comfort and discomfort. When choosing a certain behaviour, ask your body How do you feel about this? If your body sends a signal of physical or emotional distress, watch out. If your body sends a signal of comfort and eagerness, proceed.

➤ Live in the present, for it is the only moment you have. Keep your attention on what is here and now; Look for the fullness in every moment. Accept what comes to you totally and completely so that you can appreciate it, learn from it, and then let it go. The present is as it should be.

➤ Take time to be silent, to meditate, to quiet the internal dialogue. In moments of silence, realise that you are recontacting your source of pure awareness. Pay attention to your inner life so that you can be guided by intuition rather than externally imposed interpretations of what is or isn't good for you.

➤ When you find yourself reacting with anger or

opposition to any person or circumstance, realise that you are only struggling with yourself.

➢ Know that the world out there reflects your reality in here. The people you react to most strongly, whether with love or hate, are projections of your inner world. What you most hate is what you most deny in yourself. What you most love is what you most wish for in yourself. Use the mirror of relationships to guide your evolution. The goal is total self-knowledge.

➢ Shed the burden of judgement — you will feel much lighter. Judgement imposes right and wrong on situations that just are. Everything can be understood and forgiven, but when you judge, you cut off understanding and shut down the process of learning to love.

➢ Don't contaminate your body with toxins, either through food, drink, or toxic emotions. Your body is more than a life-support system. It is the vehicle that will carry you on the journey of your evolution.

➢ Replace fear — motivated behaviour with love-motivated behaviour. Fear is the product of memory, which dwells our energies toward making certain that an old hurt will not repeat itself. But trying to impose the past on the present will never wipe out the threat of being hurt.

➢ Understand that the physical world is just a mirror of a deeper intelligence. Intelligence is the invisible organiser of all matter and energy, and since a portion of this intelligence resides in you, you share in the organising power of the cosmos.

Long Hours of Working Can Kill You

A comparatively new research coming from London says that long work can kill you. A news report with the above heading was published in The Times of India dated 6th April, 2011. It was mentioned in the news story that people who regularly work long hours may be significantly increasing their risk of developing heart disease, the world's biggest killer, scientists said.

Researchers said a long-term study showed that working more than 11 hours a day increased the risk of heart disease by 67 %, compared with working a standard 7 to 8 hours a day. They said the findings suggest that information on working hours—used alongside other factors like blood pressure, diabetes and smoking habits—could help doctors work out a patient's risk of heart disease. However, they also said it was not yet clear whether long working hours themselves contribute to heart disease risk, or whether they act as a "marker" of other factors that can harm heart health—like unhealthy eating habits, a lack of exercise or depression. "This study might make us think twice about the old adage 'hard work won't kill you," said Stephen Holgate, chairman of the population and systems medicine board at Britain's Medical Research Council, which part-funded the study. The study, published in the Annals of Internal Medicine journal, followed nearly 7,100 British workers for 11 years. "Working long days is associated with a remarkable increase in risk of heart disease," said Mika Kivimaki of Britain's University College London, who led the research. He said it may be a "wake-up call for people who overwork themselves."

"People who work long hours should be particularly careful in following healthy diets, exercising sufficiently and keeping their blood pressure, cholesterol levels, and blood (sugar) within healthy limits," Kivimaki said.

How Would You Like to Be Remembered—to Decide Your Happiness

About a hundred years ago, a man looked at the morning newspaper and to this surprise and horror, read his name in the obituary column. The news papers had reported the death of the wrong person by mistake. His first response was shock. Am I here or there? When he regained his composure, his second thought was to find out what people had said about him. The obituary read, "Dynamite King Dies." And also "He was the merchant of death." This man was the inventor of dynamite and when he read the words "merchant of death," he asked himself a question, "Is this how I am going to be remembered?" He got in touch with his feelings and decided that this was not the way he wanted to be remembered. From that day on, he started working toward peace. His name was Alfred Nobel and he is remembered today by the great Nobel Prize.

Just as Alfred Nobel got in touch with his feelings and redefined his values, we should step back and do the same.

    What is your legacy?

    How would you like to be remembered?

    Will you be spoken well of?

    Will you be remembered with love and respect?

    Will you be missed?

The above actual live story as printed in Yogakshema would surely inspire us to have better quality of our own happiness.

The following God's letter for our inspiration sent to me by Brahmakumaris enables me to think and think again. This letter is known as the letter from God is as under:

    Sweet Child ....

As you got up this morning I watched you hoped you would talk to me, even if it was just a few words, asking my opinion or thanking me for something good that happened in your life yesterday—but I noticed you were too busy trying to find the right outfit to put on and wear to work. I waited again. When you ran around the house getting ready, there were a few minutes for you to stop and say hello, but you were busy. At one point you had to wait fifteen minutes with nothing to do except sit in a chair. Then, I saw you spring to your feet. I thought you wanted to talk to me but you ran to the phone and called a friend to get the latest gossip.

I watched as you went to work and I waited patiently all day long. With all your activities I guess you were too busy to say anything to me. I noticed that before lunch you looked around, may be you felt embarrassed to talk to me, that is why you didn't bow your head. You glanced three or four tables over and you noticed some of your friends talking to me briefly before they ate but you didn't. That's okay.

There is still more time left, and I had hoped that you would talk to me, yet you went 3home and it seems as if you had lots of things to do. After a few of them were done you turned on the TV, I don't know if you like TV or not, just about anything goes there and you spend a lot of time each day in front of it—thinking about anything—just enjoying the show. I waited patiently again as you watched the TV and ate your meal but again you didn't talk to me.

Bedtime—I guess you felt too tired. After you said goodnight to your family you fell into bed and went to sleep in no time. That's okay, you may not realise that I am always there for you. I've got patience, more than you will ever know. I even want to teach you how to be patient with others as well.

I love you so much that I wait every day for a nod, prayer or thought or a thankful part of your heart. It is hard to have a one-sided conversation. Well, you are getting up again and once again I will wait with nothing but love for you hoping that today you will give me some time.

Have a nice day!
Your Father and Friend .... GOD

Think and Pray for Others for Your Happiness

The following lines if remembered in true perspective would add to your happiness:

Lord, help me live from day to day
In such a self-forgetful way,
That even when I kneel to pray,
My prayer shall be for 'Others.'
Help me in all the work I do
To ever be sincere and true,
And know, that all I do for you
Must needs be done for "Others."
And when my work on earth is done,
And my new work in Heavens begun
May I forget the crown I've won,
While thinking still of 'Others.'
'Others.' Lord, Yes, 'Others!'
Let this my motto be.
Help me to live for others
That I may live for Thee.

PERSONALITY DEVELOPMENT

Management Guru Bhagwan Shri Ram
Dr. Sunil Jogi....Rs. 95

Management Guru Hanuman
Dr. Sunil Jogi....Rs. 95

Secrets Of Success Through Bhagwadgeeta
Kapil Kakkar....Rs. 95

Management Guru Chankya
Himanshu Shekha....Rs. 95

Management Guru Ganesha
B.K. Chandrashekhar
Rs. 125

Management Guru Professor Laloo's Rail
Dr. Sunil Jolgi....Rs. 150

Time Management
Dr. Rakha Vyas
Rs. 125

Be An Achiever
K G Varshney
Rs. 95

Gandhi and Management
Dr. Pravin Shukl....Rs. 95

Think And Grow Rich
Napoleon Hill
Rs. 100

Golden Sutra Of Success
P. Gopal Sharma
Rs. 95

Dare to Dream Dare to Excel
Dr. H. Devsre....Rs. 95

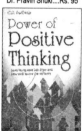

Power of Positive Thinking
G.D.Budhiraja....Rs. 95

Power to Write your Own Desting
Ashok Indu....Rs. 125

Success Is Not By Chance
Ashok Indu....Rs. 95

Think Big Become Big
Tarun Engineer....Rs. 150

 **DIAMOND BOOKS** X-30, Okhla Industrial Area, Phase-II, New Delhi-110020,
Phones : 41611861- 65, 40712100, Fax: 011- 41611866
E-mail : Sales@dpb.in, Website: www.dpb.in